YORK NOTES

ROMEO AND JULIET

WILLIAM SHAKESPEARE

NOTES BY JOHN POLLEY

 Longman   York Press

TO JUDITH

YORK PRESS
322 Old Brompton Road, London SW5 9JH

PEARSON EDUCATION LIMITED
Edinburgh Gate, Harlow,
Essex CM20 2JE, United Kingdom
Associated companies, branches and representatives throughout the world

First published 1997
This new and fully revised edition first published 2002
Sixth impression 2005

10 9 8 7 6 5

ISBN 0-582-50626-3

Designed by Michelle Cannatella
Illustrated by Tony Chance
Character Tree by Neil Gower
Typeset by Land & Unwin (Data Sciences), Bugbrooke, Northamptonshire
Produced by Pearson Education Asia Limited, Hong Kong

CONTENTS

PREFACE

York Notes are designed to give you a broader perspective on works of literature studied at GCSE and equivalent levels. With examination requirements changing in the twenty-first century, we have made a number of significant changes to this new series. We continue to help students to reach their own interpretations of the text but York Notes now have important extra-value new features.

You will discover that York Notes are genuinely interactive. The new **Checkpoint** features make sure that you can test your knowledge and broaden your understanding. You will also be directed to excellent websites, books and films where you can follow up ideas for yourself.

The **Resources** section has been updated and an entirely new section has been devoted to how to improve your grade. Careful reading and application of the principles laid out in the Resources section guarantee improved performance.

The **Detailed summaries** include an easy-to-follow skeleton structure of the story-line, while the section on **Language and style** has been extended to offer an in-depth discussion of the writer's techniques.

The Contents page shows the structure of this study guide. However, there is no need to read from the beginning to the end as you would with a novel, play or poem. Use the Notes in the way that suits you. Our aim is to help you with your understanding of the work, not to dictate how you should learn.

Our authors are practising English teachers and examiners who have used their experience to offer a whole range of **Examiner's secrets** – useful hints to encourage exam success.

The author of these Notes is John Polley. Since 1962, he has taught at grammar, comprehensive and secondary modern schools, and was a Head of English for twenty-nine years. He is currently an examiner recruiter for one of the UK's largest examination bodies.

The text used in these Notes is *Romeo and Juliet* edited by Celeste Flower in the Longman Literature Shakespeare series.

PART ONE

INTRODUCTION

HOW TO STUDY A PLAY

Though it may seem obvious, remember that a play is written to be performed before an audience. Ideally, you should see the play live on stage. A film or video recording is next best, though neither can capture the enjoyment of being in a theatre and realising that your reactions are part of the performance.

There are six aspects of a play:

❶ THE PLOT: a play is a story whose events are carefully organised by the playwright in order to show how a situation can be worked out

❷ THE CHARACTERS: these are the people who have to face this situation. Since they are human they can be good or bad, clever or stupid, likeable or detestable, etc. They may change too!

❸ THE THEMES: these are the underlying messages of the play, e.g. jealousy can cause the worst of crimes; ambition can bring the mightiest low

❹ THE SETTING: this concerns the time and place that the author has chosen for the play

❺ THE LANGUAGE: the writer uses a certain style of expression to convey the characters and ideas

❻ STAGING AND PERFORMANCE: the type of stage, the lighting, the sound effects, the costumes, the acting styles and delivery must all be decided

Work out the choices the dramatist has made in the first four areas, and consider how a director might balance these choices to create a live performance.

The purpose of these York Notes is to help you understand what the play is about and to enable you to make your own interpretation. Do not expect the study of a play to be neat and easy: plays are chosen for examination purposes, not written for them!

? DID YOU KNOW?

When studying *Romeo and Juliet* it is possible to forget that you are reading a play. If you can, go and see it performed – as Shakespeare intended!

AUTHOR – LIFE AND WORKS

1564 William Shakespeare is baptised on 26 April in Stratford-on-Avon, Warwickshire

1582 Marries Anne Hathaway

1583 Birth of daughter, Susanna

1585 Birth of twins, Hamnet and Judith

1590–93 Early published works and poems written when theatres are closed by Plague

1594 Joins Lord Chamberlain's Men (from 1603 named the King's Men) as actor and playwright

1595 *Romeo and Juliet* first performed

1595–99 Writes the history plays and comedies

1597 Shakespeare buys New Place, the second biggest house in Stratford

1599 Moves to newly-opened Globe Theatre

1599–1608 Writes his greatest plays, including *Macbeth*, *King Lear* and *Hamlet*

1608–13 Takes over the lease of Blackfriars Theatre and writes final plays, the romances, ending with *The Tempest*

1609 Shakespeare's sonnets published

1613 Globe Theatre burns down 29 June, during performance of *Henry VIII*

1616 Shakespeare dies, 23 April, and is buried in Stratford

1623 First Folio of Shakespeare's plays published

CONTEXT

1558 Elizabeth I becomes Queen of England

1568 Mary Queen of Scots is imprisoned for life

1577–80 Sir Francis Drake becomes the first to circumnavigate the world

1587 Mary Queen of Scots is executed

1588 Defeat of the Spanish Armada

1591 Tea is first drunk in England

1593–94 Outbreak of the Plague in London, closing theatres and killing as many as 5,000 people, according to some sources

1594 Queen Elizabeth spends Christmas at Greenwich and is entertained by the leading theatre company of her day, headed by James Burbage, William Kempe and Shakespeare

1595 Walter Raleigh sails to Guiana

1599 Oliver Cromwell is born

1603 Elizabeth I dies on 24 March; James I, son of Mary, succeeds to throne of England

1604 Peace treaty signed with Spain

1605 The Gunpowder Plot

1611 The Bible is translated into the Authorised (King James) Version

1614 Fire sweeps through Stratford but New Place is spared

1618 Thirty Years War begins

SETTING AND BACKGROUND

SOURCE OF THE PLAY

Shakespeare used a variety of sources for his dramas. The story of *Romeo and Juliet* was by all accounts taken from the poem, *The Tragical History of Romeus and Juliet* written by Arthur Brooke (1562) though the original story may be derived from the Greek author, Xenophon.

The play was published in quarto form in 1597 so it is safe to assume it may have been written a couple of years or so earlier, during the first stage of his career. The Quartos, so called from their format (their page size), contained single plays and were sold for sixpence apiece. If this dating is correct, this play, with its range of characters and poetry, must be reckoned his first great one.

It is, however, unusual in that it is a tragedy, for the bulk of his writing in the early years was comedies or histories.

INGREDIENTS OF A TRAGEDY

- The tragic hero should be of high, but not perfect, worth or standing.

- A tragic flaw, weakness or excess of arrogant ambition (hubris) leads to downfall.

- The effect of this, the catastrophe, on the spectators is the cleansing (catharsis) of the emotions of pity and terror through what they have witnessed.

To describe the play as a tragedy in these terms is appropriate only in part. Even if it does happen remarkably swiftly, the fact that Romeo and Juliet fall in love is hardly a tragic weakness.

Nevertheless the play is described as a tragedy and it is generally accepted that responsibility for their downfall lies outside the characters – in the workings of so-called Fate. It is the family feud rather than any moral weakness that leads to the deaths of the lovers.

CHECK THE FILM
The first film version of *Romeo and Juliet* won an Oscar for Best Film in 1936 The cast was described as 'elderly'! 'Saved – by Shakespeare – from being a bad film', said Graham Greene.

THE FRIAR AND THE WORKINGS OF FATE

Yet Fate itself is seen to be the result of divine workings: as the play nears its conclusion, Friar Lawrence reports that he has begged Juliet to leave the vault and 'bear this work of heaven with patience' (V.3.261), whilst the Prince echoes the sentiment in his final rebuke to the families that 'heaven finds means to kill your joys with love' (V.3.293). Capulet and Montague shake hands to signal the end of the feud, securing what the Friar had always sought to achieve, 'To turn [their] households' rancour to pure love' (II.3.92).

In a wider sense, the play may be viewed as a dramatic representation of the perpetual conflict between love and hatred which enmeshes a pair of unfortunate lovers. Their deaths are the inevitable outcome, so the play is a tragedy in a looser sense than a strict interpretation of Aristotle's definition would indicate.

DID YOU KNOW?

Romeo and Juliet was one of the first half-dozen plays that Shakespeare wrote.

ITALY AS A SETTING

Shakespeare chose Italy as the setting for a number of his plays. As far as one can tell, he never travelled abroad but Italy was regarded as a wealthy, romantic country where extravagant loves could properly be located. It is entirely fitting that an immortal tragedy should take as its backdrop 'fair Verona' (Prologue 2) in one of the homes of classical civilisation.

Sixteenth-century Italian **comedies** were especially high-spirited. They enjoyed the fun of sexual and social intrigue, particularly in the context of city life. Young men fall in love, often with wealthy heiresses. The Nurse's observation to Romeo (I.5.116–17), 'he that can lay hold of her / Shall have the chinks', suggests a common enough motive for love at that or any other time.

In such respects, *Romeo and Juliet* is a typical example of the European comic tradition.

GLOSSARY

chinks money
rancour enmity

Now take a break!

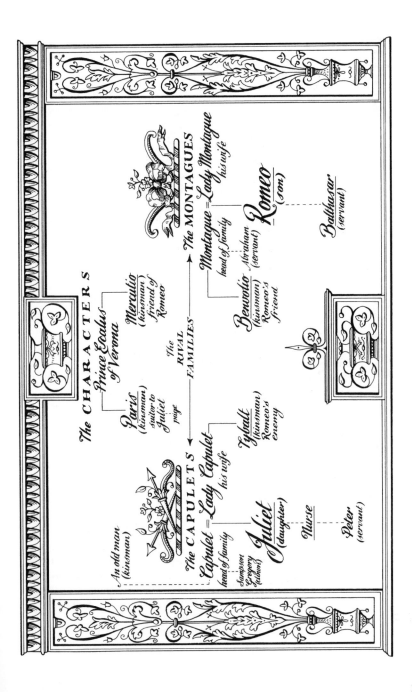

The CHARACTERS

Prince Escalus of Verona

The RIVAL FAMILIES

The MONTAGUES

Montague = Lady Montague his wife
head of family

Romeo (son)

Benvolio (kinsman) Romeo's friend

Abraham (servant)

Balthasar (servant)

Mercutio (kinsman) friend of Romeo

Paris (kinsman) suitor to Juliet
page

The CAPULETS

Capulet = Lady Capulet his wife
head of family

Juliet (daughter)

Tybalt (kinsman) Romeo's enemy

An old man (kinsman)

Sampson Gregory (servants)

Nurse

Peter (servant)

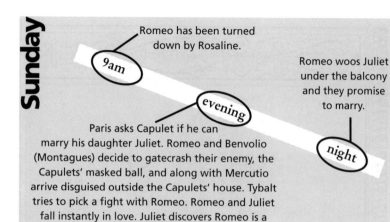

Sunday

Romeo has been turned down by Rosaline.

9am

Romeo woos Juliet under the balcony and they promise to marry.

evening

Paris asks Capulet if he can marry his daughter Juliet. Romeo and Benvolio (Montagues) decide to gatecrash their enemy, the Capulets' masked ball, and along with Mercutio arrive disguised outside the Capulets' house. Tybalt tries to pick a fight with Romeo. Romeo and Juliet fall instantly in love. Juliet discovers Romeo is a Montague.

night

Monday

Romeo asks Friar Lawrence to marry them.

Juliet hurries to meet Romeo at Friar Lawrence's.

daybreak

9am

noon

Romeo hears Tybalt wants a fight. He sends a message to Juliet to come to the Friar's cell that afternoon.

The lovers leave with him for a secret wedding, after which in a quarrel Tybalt kills Mercutio and Romeo kills Tybalt. The Prince banishes Romeo from Verona under pain of death.

afternoon

Romeo tries to kill himself, but is prevented by the Nurse. The Friar advises Romeo to spend the night with Juliet before leaving for exile in Mantua.

early evening

Juliet learns of Tybalt's death. She is desperate to see Romeo and the Nurse promises to find him.

evening

late evening

Without consulting Juliet, Capulet tells Paris he can marry her.

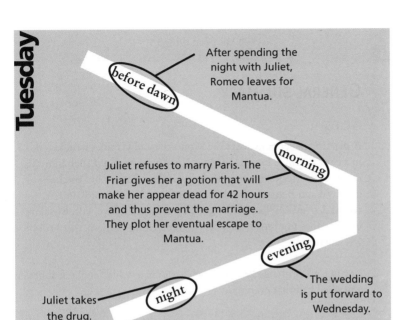

Tuesday

before dawn — After spending the night with Juliet, Romeo leaves for Mantua.

morning — Juliet refuses to marry Paris. The Friar gives her a potion that will make her appear dead for 42 hours and thus prevent the marriage. They plot her eventual escape to Mantua.

evening — The wedding is put forward to Wednesday.

night — Juliet takes the drug.

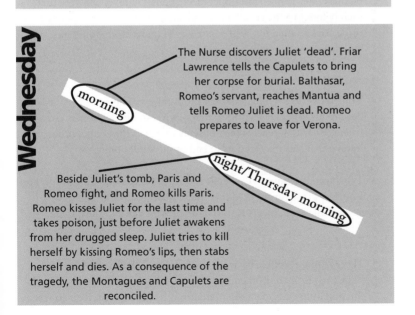

Wednesday

morning — The Nurse discovers Juliet 'dead'. Friar Lawrence tells the Capulets to bring her corpse for burial. Balthasar, Romeo's servant, reaches Mantua and tells Romeo Juliet is dead. Romeo prepares to leave for Verona.

night/Thursday morning — Beside Juliet's tomb, Paris and Romeo fight, and Romeo kills Paris. Romeo kisses Juliet for the last time and takes poison, just before Juliet awakens from her drugged sleep. Juliet tries to kill herself by kissing Romeo's lips, then stabs herself and dies. As a consequence of the tragedy, the Montagues and Capulets are reconciled.

PART TWO

SUMMARIES

GENERAL SUMMARY

ACT I

A meeting of servants from the Montague and Capulet families ends in a brawl. Prince Escalus threatens dire punishment if such fighting recurs. The Montagues are pleased that their Romeo has not been involved and Benvolio is asked to discover the cause of Romeo's recent depression. Romeo reveals he has fallen in love with Rosaline but she does not return his affections. Benvolio suggests that he look elsewhere.

CHECK THE NET
www.shakespeare.
sk gives the complete works of Shakespeare with a glossary.

Lord Capulet invites Paris who wishes to marry his daughter, Juliet, to a masked ball that evening.

Romeo learns of the ball and decides to gatecrash since Rosaline will be there. But Romeo and Juliet meet and fall in love, unaware that each belongs to the rival family. Tybalt, Lady Capulet's nephew, recognises Romeo but is prevented by Capulet from doing him violence.

ACT II

Romeo overhears Juliet talking on the balcony and steps forward to declare his love. They agree to marry without delay. Romeo visits his friend, Friar Lawrence, who consents to marry the couple in secret, hoping that this may lead to an end of the family feud.

Tybalt sends Romeo a challenge to a duel. Juliet's nurse arrives to hear Romeo's plans for the wedding. Juliet manages to leave her house to go to confession, meets Romeo at the Friar's cell and they are married.

ACT III

There is more trouble between the families. Tybalt is looking for a fight with Romeo. Romeo steps between him and Mercutio to stop them fighting. Accidentally Mercutio is fatally injured. Romeo reacts violently. He fights and kills Tybalt. The Prince is again involved and sentences Romeo to immediate banishment. Romeo has gone to Friar Lawrence where they are joined by the Nurse. They plan to smuggle Juliet to Mantua to be reunited with the banished Romeo. Juliet and Romeo enjoy their only night together and he flees. Capulet and Paris arrange for Juliet to marry Paris.

ACT IV

Juliet finds her Nurse has now turned against her. The Friar comes up with a scheme for Juliet to go along with her parents' plans but the night before the wedding to take a drug that will put her into a state of suspended animation. She will be placed in the family vault whilst the Friar arranges for Romeo to rescue her. Juliet does as he suggests, then takes the drug and her body is discovered exactly as the Friar had intended.

ACT V

Balthasar, Romeo's servant, rushes to Mantua with news of Juliet's death. Distraught, Romeo buys poison from an apothecary and hurries back to be with Juliet. The Friar learns that his message has not reached Romeo and sets off to the tomb to release her. Romeo arrives there first. He is challenged by Paris, who dies in a vain attempt to prevent Romeo from getting into the vault. He sees the still-drugged Juliet and takes the fatal poison. Juliet revives to discover Romeo dead beside her. The Friar has eventually arrived though he is unsuccessful in his efforts to make Juliet leave the vault. Fearful of the consequences for himself, he leaves and Juliet stabs herself.

The Montagues, Capulets and the Prince arrive at the tragic scene. The Friar describes the story of the lovers' romance, uniting both families in their grief. At last they realise the futile misery of their family feud and resolve to end it.

 CHECK THE FILM
The two top Shakespearean films were both versions of *Romeo and Juliet*: *Romeo + Juliet* (1996) by Baz Luhrmann; and *Romeo and Juliet* (1968) by Franco Zefirelli.

DETAILED SUMMARIES

PROLOGUE

❶ The story is to be a love affair.

❷ The lovers are from feuding families.

❸ The feud ends with their deaths.

The Prologue tells us that the deaths of the 'star-crossed lovers' (line 6) is the only way their 'parents' rage' (line 10) will end. The knowledge of their certain death adds pathos to our view of events. The Prologue takes the form of a **sonnet**, a characteristic form of love poetry.

 DID YOU KNOW?

After *Romeo and Juliet*, Shakespeare did not write another tragedy for some time; Julius Caesar followed four or five years later: c.1599.

The story of the play

The Prologue tells us the story in advance. This foreknowledge allows the audience an overview of the actions of Romeo and Juliet: we can see them struggling to attain happiness and know that they are always doomed to fail – in this life at least.

SCENE 1 – Trouble on the streets

❶ A fight breaks out between servants of the Montague and Capulet families.

❷ Benvolio, a Montague, tries to stop the trouble but Tybalt, a Capulet, makes matters worse by setting on him.

❸ Prince Escalus arrives and stops the trouble, warning that the feuding must end on pain of death.

❹ Lord and Lady Montague are relieved that Romeo is not involved and ask Benvolio to find out why he has been so miserable.

❺ Romeo reveals to Benvolio that he is in love with Rosaline but that she does not love him in return.

❻ Romeo dismisses Benvolio's suggestion to look for a different woman to love.

> **CHECKPOINT 1**
>
> How does Shakespeare bring out the differences between Tybalt and Benvolio?

The running battle between the families establishes the notion of the family feud whilst the coarseness of the servants' language contrasts sharply with the purity of Romeo and Juliet's love affair. The appearance of the Prince brings things to an abrupt ending but the families are unable to control the violence until they themselves realise where their violence leads.

Tybalt's first appearance, 'Have at thee, coward!' (line 69) establishes him as one who enjoys a fight. Romeo is absent from the fight, much to the relief of his parents. They are worried about his apparent depression and request his best friend, Benvolio, to use his close friendship to discover what is the matter with him.

Romeo's fit of depression brought on by his unrequited love would have been perfectly understandable to Shakespeare's audience: love was meant to be a painful matter! Romeo is suffering from what is called **Petrarchan** love. Here the lover postures and displays lovesickness, whilst the object of his love adopts a cool and disdainful attitude towards him.

The love affair of Romeo and Juliet is to be played out against a background of hatred. Benvolio is a good man yet even he dismisses Romeo's strong feelings and suggests he look elsewhere.

> **GLOSSARY**
>
> **star-crossed** bound to fail since their destiny was determined by the stars
>
> **their parents' rage** the feud between the families
>
> **Have at thee, coward!** a challenge to a fight

Romeo describes his feelings (lines 169–81) with the use of oxymoron, e.g. 'cold fire', and antithesis which are typical of poems written in the Petrarchan tradition.

Benvolio's advice to look at other girls , 'Examine other beauties' (line 226), is naturally rejected by Romeo, though ironically it is precisely what is to happen.

SCENE 2 – Juliet's future considered

1️⃣ Capulet discusses Paris's proposal to marry Juliet.

2️⃣ Capulet invites Paris to a masked ball that evening to see Juliet.

3️⃣ They may marry if Juliet agrees.

4️⃣ The Clown is entrusted with a list of the guests.

5️⃣ Unable to read, he asks Romeo and Benvolio to help him decipher it.

6️⃣ Romeo sees Rosaline's name amongst the guests and resolves to go to the ball.

Paris's proposal to marry Juliet is conducted with her parents and it seems as though Lord Capulet is reluctant to agree to an early marriage. Juliet's age did not at that time necessarily rule out marriage though Capulet would have preferred his only daughter to have been a couple of years older since she is a 'stranger in the world' (line 8).

CHECKPOINT 2

Is Capulet a concerned father?

Paris's suggestion that there are younger mothers in Verona is echoed later (I.2.67–71) by Lady Capulet who reveals that she was married at a similarly early age herself.

Capulet's advice to Paris to compare Juliet with other girls at the masked ball is strikingly similar to that just given by Benvolio (I.1.225–6). His decision to entrust the list of guests to one of his servants, the Clown, seems natural but it is the beginning of a chain of events that will bring Romeo and Juliet together.

The chance meeting with the Clown presents Benvolio with the opportunity to urge Romeo to forget Rosaline by comparing her with 'all the admired beauties of Verona' (line 87).

Love and fate

Capulet is naturally keen that his daughter should find a considerate husband and goes along with Paris's proposal, provided it meets with Juliet's approval. Later in the play his attitude has changed and he forces Juliet into marriage.

Fate plays a hand in arranging that the servant with the guest list is illiterate. It therefore seems quite natural that he should seek help in reading the names – and that Romeo is there to do just that!

SCENE 3 – Juliet's mother gives some advice

1 Lady Capulet talks to Juliet about Paris's proposal of marriage.

2 Juliet's Nurse gives a longwinded – and explicit – explanation of how she knows Juliet is nearly fourteen years of age.

3 Lady Capulet tells her daughter that Paris intends to come to the ball, making it plain that she is keen for a relationship to develop.

4 Juliet responds guardedly that she will look at him but do nothing without her mother's consent.

The women of the Montague household now discuss Paris's proposal of marriage. The closeness of Juliet's relationship with the Nurse is indicated by the description of how she was wet-nursed. Lady Caupulet is rather impatient with the Nurse because she wishes to impress on her daughter that Paris's offer is a very attractive one. The desire for her to marry comes across plainly in the blunt question, 'How stands your dispositions to be married?' (line 63).

> **GLOSSARY**
>
> **Feather of lead, bright smoke, cold fire** examples of oxymoron typical of the Petrarchan or courtly lover
>
> **Examine other beauties** look at other women
>
> **A stranger in the world** still quite young
>
> **How stands your dispositions to be married** Would you like to marry?

Lady Capulet is keen to impress on her daughter that she was a mother herself at 'a pretty age' (line 11). The Nurse is excited by the prospect of Juliet marrying Paris.

Lady Capulet's advice is very different from that given by the men: Juliet is not to compare Paris with anyone, just look at him very closely! The secene ends with Julet excited at the prospect of the evening ahead and her mother tolerably satisfied that her daughter will soon be married to a wealthy man.

> **Lady Capulet and marriage**
>
> Lady Capulet is far more keen than her husband on her daughter marrying. She herself was married young so Juliet's youth is not a problem. The later pressure on Juliet to marry Paris may be initiated by her and would account for her husband's apparent change of attitude towards Juliet.

SCENE 4 – The Montagues go to the ball

❶ The Montague family, including Romeo, Benvolio and Mercutio, makes its way to the ball.

CHECKPOINT 3

Does Mercutio's attitude towards love differ from that of Romeo?

❷ Mercutio is in a very good humour, enjoying himself as he teases Romeo for being moody and unadventurous.

❸ Romeo remains anxious, feeling that something terrible may be about to happen tonight.

The men make their way to the masked ball in high spirits in much the way all young people at all times look forward to a good night out. Romeo is going reluctantly to the ball, though he is happy to parade the misery of the love he feels. Mercutio's 'Queen Mab' speech is part of his tactic to persuade Romeo to enter into the fun of the evening. He describes the sensual effect that Queen Mab has upon women. More importantly Mercutio enables the audience to see that Romeo's attitude to his present love amounts to nothing more than a pose: this matters since Romeo has really to fall in love with Juliet.

Romeo's glum assertion that he feels something awful is about to overtake him (lines 107–12) echoes the 'star-crossed lovers' referred to in the first Prologue (line 6).

www. CHECK
THE NET
www.geocities.com
/area51/1044/
queenmab.htm
for more about
faeries

Romeo's premonition

Romeo is not cheered up by Mercutio's banter. He is going to see Rosaline but has a feeling that something is about to happen that 'blows us from ourselves' (line 105), stopping him from seeing her. He asks the forces of fate to help him, 'But He that hath the steerage of my course, / Direct my sail' (lines 113–14). Romeo fears that 'Some consequence, yet hanging in the stars' (line 108) may lead to his death.

SCENE 5 – Romeo and Juliet meet at the ball

❶ Capulet welcomes his guests before sitting down with an aged cousin to watch the fun.

❷ Romeo suddenly sees Juliet, and is smitten by her beauty.

❸ Tybalt overhears Romeo talking. Enraged by a Montague gatecrasher, he sends for his sword.

❹ Capulet defends Romeo and Tybalt leaves, promising future trouble.

❺ Romeo and Juliet meet for the first time. It is love at first sight as the two share a sonnet and kisses.

❻ Romeo is told that Juliet is a Capulet; Juliet discovers from the Nurse that Romeo is a Montague.

The scene starts on a light-hearted note as Capulet offers a rambling welcome to his guests (lines 15–32). Romeo's response to Juliet's beauty is instant: she literally dazzles him and it comes out in his

GLOSSARY

pretty age right for marriage

Queen Mab queen of the fairies and bringer of dreams

blows us from ourselves deflects us from our purposes

consequence, yet hanging in the stars event destined to happen

Scene 5 continued

language (lines 44–9). By chance Tybalt overhears Romeo's comment and reacts viciously. His response to Romeo's presence is important in the overall context of the play, as is the stinging rebuke he receives from Capulet. He is obliged to leave the ball, swearing for revenge.

Romeo and Juliet's first meeting is handled most unusually. They take the floor for a dance and in their opening words they share a sonnet (lines 93–106). It is an appropriate and original choice of words: the Prologue to the play has employed the same device. Apart for a few moments at the end of the scene, the two lovers reveal to us their reactions to the meeting.

CHECKPOINT 4

How does Tybalt's cry for revenge at the very moment when the lovers meet bear out Romeo's premonition in the last scene?

Love at first sight

The meeting of the lovers has to be sensational. Shakespeare conveys their opening words to each other in the form of a sonnet which they share and create. This sonnet has a beauty and formality which perfectly capture the awkwardness yet irresistibility of the moment. The central image – of a pilgrim worshipping at a shrine – underlines the depth and purity of their love. The love they share is far from the Petrarchan expression of the notion we have seen in Act I, Scene 1.

The subsequent discovery that each belongs to a rival family serves to make their love that much more poignant. Romeo, in particular, senses that his love for Juliet may have darker implications when he talks of the 'Prodigious birth of love' (140).

 CHECK THE FILM

Notice how their meeting is handled in the 1968 Franco Zeffirelli production.

There is a grim truth in Juliet's view that her 'grave is like to be [her] wedding bed' (line 135). Juliet's indirectness in telling the Nurse which man interests her displays her youth and shyness.

Now take a break!

WHO SAYS ...?

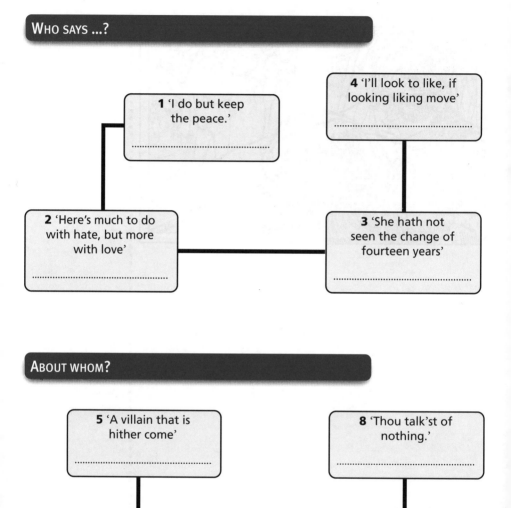

1 'I do but keep the peace.'

....

2 'Here's much to do with hate, but more with love'

....

3 'She hath not seen the change of fourteen years'

....

4 'I'll look to like, if looking liking move'

....

ABOUT WHOM?

5 'A villain that is hither come'

....

6 'This night you shall behold him at our feast'

....

7 ''A bears him like a portly gentleman'

....

8 'Thou talk'st of nothing.'

....

Check your answers on p. 85.

THE PROLOGUE GIVES AN UPDATE

❶ Romeo has now forgotten his love for Rosaline and has fallen head-over-heels in love with Juliet.

By now we can appreciate how appropriate it is for the Chorus to use a sonnet to describe the progress of Romeo's love. Happily the lovers are able to temper 'extremities with extreme sweet' (line 14).

SCENE 1 – Later Sunday night

❶ Mercutio and Benvolio are looking for Romeo.

Mercutio and Benvolio search for Romeo after the ball. They still believe he is in love with Rosaline and after a few coarse remarks decide that he does not want to be found since they have seen him scale an orchard wall. Benvolio seems rather strait-laced in his language: he is concerned to find out his cousin's reaction to the ball. He has, after all, been charged by Romeo's parents to find out his state of mind.

Mercutio is more than a little blunt with his sexual references. His view of the relations between the sexes contrasts sharply with the purity of the love vows so recently exchanged by Romeo and Juliet.

Mercutio, of course, still believes that it is Rosaline whom Romeo loves.

CHECKPOINT 5

Has Mercutio's idea of Romeo's love changed?

GLOSSARY

tempering extremities with extreme sweet easing the difficulties of their relationship with extreme pleasure

---

SCENE 2 – The Lovers meet in the orchard

1 Romeo has slipped away from his friends to the Capulets' orchard.

2 Overhearing Juliet on her balcony pledging her love for him, he steps forward to reveal his presence.

3 She recognises him immediately and warns him of the dangers he is taking by being there.

4 The lovers exchange vows.

5 Juliet tells Romeo to make arrangements for their marriage: she will send the Nurse to him the next day to find out what he has planned.

CHECKPOINT 6

What does Juliet mean by the word *wherefore* in the line, 'Wherefore art thou Romeo?'

The fact that so many famous quotations are taken from this scene indicates the quality of the poetry in this meeting of the lovers.

Romeo stands hidden from Juliet in her garden till the light from her opening window and the appearance of Juliet herself draws him forward.

Just as Romeo had been dazzled by his first view of Juliet, so here in the opening lines she is perceived as a source of light (lines 2–22). Juliet's first concern is for his safety (lines 64–5). Her next is that he may feel she is too forward (lines 85–106). The lovers are given ample time to pledge their vows until they are finally interrupted by a repeated call from the Nurse.

The protracted farewell – Juliet comes and goes twice from the balcony – is a charming way of conveying the excitement that she is feeling and leads comfortably into the famous line 'Parting is such sweet sorrow' (line 184).

The declaration of love

Juliet's declaration of love to herself is a convenient dramatic device. It speeds up the action and Romeo is thereby free to step forward, announce his presence and immediately pledge his love.

SCENE 3 – The Friar agrees to the marriage

1 Friar Lawrence is in his cell sorting through various herbs he has picked.

2 Romeo enters with a request to conduct a wedding ceremony for him.

3 The Friar, surprised to learn that Romeo is not intending to marry Rosaline, condemns the fickleness of men.

4 Nevertheless he agrees to Romeo's request, if only because it may lead to a reconciliation between the opposing families.

EXAMINER'S SECRET
You will not get high marks simply by retelling the story.

The Friar appears with a basket of herbs he has been picking. His discussion of the various qualities of plants that he has picked prepares us for his later use of them to solve Verona's problems, turning their 'households' rancour to pure love' (line 92). He is an expert and later we are able to believe that he has discovered a drug that will enable Juliet to enter a state of suspended animation.

GLOSSARY
rancour bitter enmity

DID YOU KNOW?

The story of *Romeo and Juliet* has been used for three operas: *Capuletti e i Montecchi* (Vincenzo Bellini, 1830); *Romeo and Juliet* (Charles Gounod, 1867); *A Village Romeo and Juliet* (Frederick Delius, 1907).

Romeo has come straight from his passionate meeting with Juliet and blurts out immediately that he wants the Friar to arrange a wedding for him. Romeo's changing affections give ample opportunity for the Friar to make some heavy moral points about the fickleness of men in general (line 80).

The reference back to the nature of Romeo's love for Rosaline is a useful reminder of the difference in his love for Juliet. The Friar has identified that Romeo's love for Rosaline was 'doting' (line 82).

What prompts the Friar to agree to marry Romeo and Juliet is his conviction that this may settle the differences between the two families (lines 90–2).

The Friar's role in the play

The Friar is a respected figure in the play. His advice is sought by Romeo, the Nurse and Paris. This gives him a pivotal position, as he sees it, in being able to unite the feuding families by a strategic marriage, and thereby to bring peace to the streets of Verona.

SCENE 4 – The details of the marriage are agreed

1 Mercutio and Benvolio have learnt that Tybalt has sent a challenge to Romeo.

2 Romeo arrives and they make fun of him for deserting them to go to his lady love.

3 The Nurse enters and, after some lewd comments from Mercutio, takes Romeo aside and assures him that Juliet loves him.

4 Romeo sends the message that Juliet is to come to Friar Lawrence's cell that afternoon where they will be married.

We meet the Montague men discussing the events of the night before and considering what is to be done about Tybalt. Mercutio reveals a healthy contempt for Tybalt (lines 20–36) which indicates that if Romeo will not take up the challenge, it will not pass unregarded.

The witty exchange between Romeo and his friends shows how much he has already changed from the miserable, lovesick young man we met at the beginning of the play. Benvolio underlines the change in lines 86–90, 'now art thou Romeo'.

Mercutio's ribald jests about sex (again!) contrast sharply with the true love Romeo and Juliet have found. The entry of the Nurse gives Mercutio a new opportunity to make some personal comments. She is, of course, a member of the Capulet household and as such a fair target for a spot of personal abuse. Romeo sends them ahead so that he can talk to the Nurse on his own.

Initially, he is a little nonplussed by the Nurse's apparent stupidity (lines 155–71) though he is purposeful and businesslike in ensuring that Juliet receives the correct message.

The wedding plans are fixed

Romeo is still having to contend with his friends' jests about his amorous intentions but he will not be deflected. The Nurse jokes with him as well but he replies earnestly, determined that the wedding plans will be finalised.

> **CHECKPOINT 7**
>
> Is Romeo's love for Juliet changing him?

> **GLOSSARY**
> **doting** infatuated

SCENE 5 – The Nurse gives Juliet the good news

❶ In the Capulets' garden, Juliet anxiously awaits the return of the Nurse.

❷ When she arrives, the Nurse takes delight in keeping Juliet in suspense over Romeo's message.

❸ Eventually, to Juliet's obvious relief, the Nurse reveals what Romeo has said.

Juliet is waiting impatiently for the return of the Nurse, and this impatience itself offers a charming insight into the innocence of her nature.

CHECKPOINT 8

How are Juliet's feelings revealed in the opening lines of the scene?

The Nurse enjoys the power of the news she is carrying. She deliberately refuses to offer straight answers. Juliet reacts towards the Nurse's delayed response in just the way Romeo has done in the previous scene, though the news that Romeo has made the arrangements is consequently received with far greater joy.

The role of the Nurse

The Nurse occupies a similar position in Juliet's life to the Friar in Romeo's. She enjoys her power over Juliet which is illustrated in her teasing. The Friar too enjoys teasing Romeo as he does earlier on in this Act. However, unlike the Friar, the Nurse does not have a public position, so when things go wrong, she lacks the courage to face the consequences of her actions.

SCENE 6 – The Wedding

❶ Romeo awaits Juliet's arrival at the Friar's cell.

❷ The Friar expresses his misgivings about the suddenness of Romeo's decision to marry.

3 Juliet enters, and after a loving exchange, they retire with Friar Lawrence to be married.

DID YOU KNOW?

The end of this scene makes a convenient break for the interval in most modern productions.

This is a a short and beautiful scene which covers the last moments before the lovers are married.

The Friar's apprehensions about the suddenness of Romeo and Juliet's love, 'violent delights' which have 'violent ends' (line 9), remind us of the words of the Prologue to Act I.

The last fourteen lines of the scene amount to an exchange of vows between the two. It lacks only the rhyme scheme of a sonnet although the final couplet goes to the Friar as he whisks them away to the (unseen) altar.

Married at last

There is no celebration of the marriage on stage for unlike a conventional love story the climax of this tale is not the marriage of the young couple.

GLOSSARY
These violent delights have violent ends Lovers' passions are shortlived

Now take a break!

WHO SAYS ...?

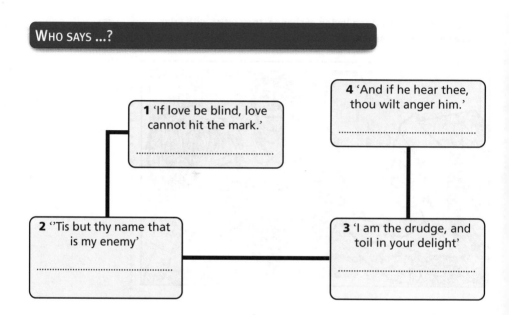

1 'If love be blind, love cannot hit the mark.'

....

4 'And if he hear thee, thou wilt anger him.'

....

2 ''Tis but thy name that is my enemy'

....

3 'I am the drudge, and toil in your delight'

....

ABOUT WHOM?

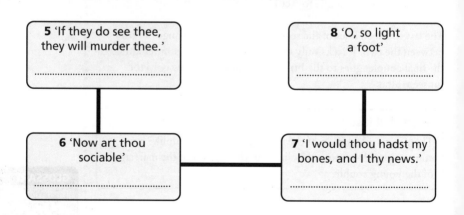

5 'If they do see thee, they will murder thee.'

....

8 'O, so light a foot'

....

6 'Now art thou sociable'

....

7 'I would thou hadst my bones, and I thy news.'

....

Check your answers on p. 85.

SCENE 1 – Back on the streets of Verona

1 Mercutio, Benvolio and various attendants meet in the street, aware of the trouble brewing this hot day.

2 Tybalt appears looking for Romeo and the opportunity for a fight.

3 Romeo joins the group fresh from his wedding.

4 He tries to avoid conflict with Tybalt but Mercutio, mistaking his reluctance for cowardice, starts to fence with Tybalt.

5 Romeo steps between them to stop the fight but Mercutio is accidentally and fatally wounded and Tybalt flees.

6 When Tybalt returns, an incensed Romeo fights and kills Tybalt, then flees.

7 The Prince sentences Romeo in his absence to immediate banishment on pain of death.

EXAMINER'S SECRET

If the rubric gives planning time, **use it** to plan your answers!

There is something familiar about the opening of this scene: it is a hot day and the men of both households are out looking for trouble.

Benvolio is playing his accustomed role as a peacemaker trying to persuade Mercutio to come home and avoid trouble. Mercutio, as usual, will not listen.

He is almost fighting with Tybalt when Romeo arrives from the wedding and is enraged by Romeo's reluctance to draw swords with Tybalt. His challenge to Tybalt as 'King of Cats' (line 76) recalls his slighting reference to him (II.4.20). Romeo tries to stop Mercutio and Tybalt fighting and in the confusion Mercutio receives a fatal stab wound. He dies in Romeo's arms with the haunting curse 'A plague o' both your houses', (line 106) a curse that is soon to be carried out. His death effectively puts an end to the Friar's plan to reunite simply the warring families.

CHECKPOINT 9

Why does Mercutio fight with Tybalt?

When Tybalt returns, Romeo now feels that he must fight Tybalt to avenge his friend Mercutio and to prove that his love for Juliet has not softened him. Both things give his fighting a power that is enough to beat Tybalt, yet even as Tybalt dies he realises the consequences of what he has done: 'I am fortune's fool' (line 136), he immediately declares. Although we know that he and Juliet are fated to die, we still hope against hope that the workings of fate might be thwarted – and time and again we are disappointed. Here is one of those occasions: just when everything is going so well, Romeo is caught up against his will in a series of events that shatter the happiness.

The fatal fight

Romeo is drawn into the fight much against his will. His marriage to Juliet has, in fact, started the reconciliation process between the two families. But a far more basic instinct – the desire of a man to avoid being thought a coward – prevails and Romeo is driven to fight Tybalt.

Benvolio's truthful account of the fight is seen as biased by the Capulets but it causes the Prince to retreat from his previously hard line on the punishment for 'civil brawls' (I.1.87). The sentence of banishment on Romeo leaves open the possibility of a happy ending.

As in the opening scene of the play, it falls to the Prince to subdue the fighting and try to restore sense to the proceedings. He listens to Benvolio's account of the fatal struggle (lines 152–75) which understandably appears slightly coloured by his kinship to Romeo.

Still it is worth noting that in an attempt to achieve balance he terms both Mercutio and Tybalt 'stout' (lines 169, 173).

The Prince has had enough bloodshed so does not condemn Romeo to death, though he does view banishment as a severe penalty: he points out that 'Mercy but murders' (line 197) since it is no deterrent.

SCENE 2 – Juliet hears the news

1 Juliet impatiently awaits her husband to join her on their wedding night.

2 The Nurse enters grief-stricken with the news of Tybalt's death.

3 She tell Juliet that Romeo is to be banished from Verona.

4 She agrees to fetch Romeo from Friar Lawrence so that the lovers can spend the night together.

Meanwhile, Juliet is awaiting her new husband, blissfully unaware of the events unfolding elsewhere. Her eagerness for night to come clearly proceeds from a desire to consummate the marriage, in marked comparison with Rosaline's attitude to Romeo.

Towards the end of the soliloquy, Juliet likens Romeo to a source of light, and then ironically – remember the Prologue's 'star-crossed lovers' (I.Prologue.6) – suggests cutting him out 'in little stars' (line 22) when she dies.

When Juliet learns from the Nurse that Romeo has caused the death of Tybalt, her confusion is shown through oxymoron, 'A damnèd saint, an honourable villain' (line 79). It takes the Nurse to shout 'Shame come to Romeo!' (line 90) to bring Juliet to his defence.

The gravity of the sentence of exile is apparent in Juliet's grief at the knowledge that Romeo is to be banished. She fears she may be 'maiden-widowèd' (line 135).

CHECKPOINT 10

What feelings come across in Juliet's opening speech: 'maiden-widowed with my husband gone before our wedding-night'

GLOSSARY

King of Cats Cats were often called Tyb in Shakespeare's time, short for Tybby and Tybalt

A plague o' both your houses May both Capulets and Montagues go to hell!

I am fortune's fool Fate is simply playing with me

civil brawls public fights

stout brave

Her only comfort comes at the end of the scene when the Nurse agrees to fetch Romeo to spend the night with Juliet.

This is the last occasion on which the Nurse puts her love for Juliet before her personal safety. It is clear that she feels less for Romeo than for Tybalt.

SCENE 3 – The Friar proposes a rescue plan

❶ In the Friar's cell, a distraught Romeo learns that the Prince has sentenced him to exile.

❷ The Nurse enters with news of Juliet's misery and Romeo desperately draws his dagger to kill himself.

❸ Furiously the Friar stops him.

❹ He quickly devises a scheme for Romeo to go to Mantua, where eventually the Friar will be able to arrange some sort of reunion.

CHECKPOINT 11

Why is the Friar
keen to help the
lovers?

Romeo is in the Friar's cell unaware of the sentence passed on him by the Prince. It falls to the Friar to inform him of 'the Prince's doom' (lines 4, 9).

Romeo's response to news of his banishment echoes that of Juliet moments earlier. He is given to sudden mood changes: he did after all fall violently in love with Juliet, so the violence of his reaction to being separated is consistent with his character.

The Friar's initial suggestion is that Romeo should look to philosophy. As an older man, he is able to find comfort in questioning the eternal truths.

Driven to despair, Romeo echoes Juliet's words (II.2.40–42), 'What's Montague?...' as he asks the Friar where in his body that name resides (lines 104–6).

The Friar's scheme in this scene for the lovers to communicate at a distance and wait for a change of the social climate in Verona seems quite a plausible one.

The Friar's dilemma

The Friar feels responsible for what has happened and desperately seeks a way out of the dilemma. In fact, there is no real need for anyone to do anything at this stage; certainly he will not be able to 'reverse a Prince's doom' (line 59). Time will pass and Romeo may be forgiven. Then they will be able 'to blaze [their] marriage' (line 150).

SCENE 4 – THE Capulet reaction to the death of Tybalt

❶ The Capulets discuss with Paris the strength of Juliet's reaction to the news of Tybalt's death.

❷ They decide that her wedding with Paris should be arranged as soon as possible.

❸ Lady Capulet is told to give Juliet the message that the wedding will take place in three days' time.

Capulet abandons his earlier indulgence towards Juliet. He believes that she will agree to his 'desperate tender' (line 12) to marry Paris. The discussion about Juliet's reaction to the death of Tybalt settles on the decision that the marriage will take place as quickly as possible – in the next seventy-two hours. It will be a quiet affair with Tybalt so recently dead so that people would not think they 'held him carelessly' (line 25).

A hasty marriage

Arrangements for the hasty marriage are unobtrusively introduced but add greater momentum to the pace of events. The audience has the feeling that it is rushing towards a swift conclusion of the story. The decision to force a quick marriage also rules out the the solution just proposed by the Friar: that Romeo wait in Mantua till the social climate changes.

GLOSSARY

reverse a Prince's doom change his sentence

blaze [their] marriage make it public

desperate tender daring offer

held him carelessly did not care much for him

DID YOU KNOW?

The best-known ballet interpretation of *Romeo and Juliet* is that of Sergei Prokofiev, first danced in Moscow in 1935.

SCENE 5 – The lovers' parting

❶ The lovers are at the bedroom window, each putting off the moment of their final separation.

❷ The Nurse arrives with news that Lady Capulet is coming to see Juliet. They part.

❸ Lady Capulet greets the weeping Juliet with unexpected arrangements for the wedding with Paris.

❹ Juliet refuses point-blank to cooperate.

❺ Her enraged father gives her a final choice: marriage or ejection from his house.

❻ Juliet looks for guidance and comfort from the Nurse who tells her to forget Romeo and marry Paris.

❼ Juliet realises that only the Friar, to whom she is now going, can help her.

The final parting is staged in very much the same way as the balcony scene (II.2), neatly rounding off their meeting. The position of the lovers during the closing words (lines 48–58) also anticipates the final moments of Juliet's life (V.3). Romeo leaves in much the way that he first left Juliet – on the balcony. The entrance of Lady Capulet brings an abrupt end to Juliet's sadness over her loss of Romeo as she is now hurtled into an impossible marriage.

Lady Capulet's intended vengeance for Romeo (lines 86–91) bears similarities to the Friar's scheme for Romeo. **Ironically**, her plan includes giving Romeo a poison that will lead to him keeping Tybalt company.

Capulet enters expecting the news of the early wedding to have settled Juliet's grieving for Tybalt, and his first words show sympathy for her supposed weeping (lines 125–37). This is quickly replaced by an almost incoherent rage when he realises that Juliet will not obey him (lines 148–67).

Lady Capulet's response is predictably angry: right from the start she has wanted her daughter to marry Paris.

Juliet is left with an impossible ultimatum – marry Paris or be thrown out of the family. She turns to her remaining friend, the Nurse, for comfort. The Nurse's advice to Juliet (lines 211–25) reveals her weakness of character. Were the details of the marriage to become common knowledge, her position would be difficult in the extreme. Yet her comparison of Romeo, a 'dishclout' (line 219), with Paris, 'he's a lovely gentleman!' (line 218), seems rather over the top!

Juliet is left alone

We skip the wedding night to concentrate on the lovers' final parting. This is delivered by means of a passage of elevated poetry, an **aubade** which has the effect of heightening the emotions. Juliet's feelings descend dramatically in this scene. When the scene opens, she feels loved and complete. By the end, she has been deserted by everyone.

At the key moment, her faith in a loving father is dashed by his absolute insistence upon a swift marriage to Paris. Betrayal by her remaining friend, the Nurse, leaves her no option. 'Thou and my bosom henceforth shall be twain', she says (line 240), and turns to the Friar.

> **CHECKPOINT 12**
> Why is Lady Capulet not surprised to find her daughter weeping?

> **GLOSSARY**
> **dishclout** a dishcloth
> **thou and my bosom henceforth shall be twain** From now on you will not share my secrets

Scene 5 continued

By the end of their conversation Juliet knows she is alone. She reassures the Nurse that she is sorry that she has 'displeased' her father and is about to seek forgiveness from the Friar (lines 231–3). Left alone, she expresses her hatred of the Nurse and her intention to find 'remedy' (line 241) from the Friar.

 DID YOU KNOW?

Oscar Wilde once said: 'We become lovers when we see *Romeo and Juliet*, and *Hamlet* makes us students'.

Now take a break!

WHO SAYS ...?

4 'He shall not make me there a joyful bride.'

....

1 'For now, these hot days, is the mad blood stirring.'

....

2 'I do protest I never injured thee'

....

3 'They have made worms' meat of me.'

....

ABOUT WHOM?

5 'Affection makes him false'

....

8 'Thou has comforted me marvellous much.'

....

6 'Take him and cut him out in little stars'

....

7 'Peace, you mumbling fool!'

....

Check your answers on p. 85.

SCENE 1 – Juliet turns to the Friar

❶ At the Friar's cell, Paris seeks advice about his forthcoming wedding.

❷ Juliet arrives and Paris respects Juliet's desire for privacy by taking his leave.

CHECK THE BOOK
Joan Lingard's novel, *Across the Barricades* (1975), brings the plight of Romeo and Juliet into the modern day, with its tale of forbidden love in Northern Ireland.

❸ Juliet reveals the depth of her despair – she produces a knife and offers to kill herself.

❹ The Friar comes up with a scheme that she is prepared to put into practice.

❺ Juliet departs with the drug, as the Friar composes a letter for Romeo to explain what is happening.

Paris is talking to the Friar about the wedding arrangements. He briefly meets Juliet as she arrives looking for the Friar's help to avoid just that happening.

Paris is aware that Juliet may not love him: he has not even broached the subject, he tells the Friar, particularly since Tybalt's death when he sensibly observes, 'Venus smiles not in a house of tears' (line 8). When Paris meets Juliet now, she gives him a dusty response. His predicament here seems very similar to that in which Romeo found himself at the beginning of the play, a man whose love is not requited.

Juliet's conversation with Friar Lawrence is quite desperate and the Friar has to physically restrain her from stabbing herself to death. His approach to her misery is in marked contrast with that of the Nurse. He is aware that a second wedding is impossible and that a practical solution is required. He produces a 'vial' (line 93), containing the drug that will solve all the problems. His scheme is far-fetched but the pressure of events requires desperate remedies.

> ### The rescue plan
>
> The Friar's plan is that tomorrow night, Wednesday, Juliet will drink a concoction which will induce in her a state of suspended animation for forty-two hours. She will be taken to the Capulets' vault. The Friar will send a message to Romeo in Mantua via a fellow friar so that he can come to rescue her when she awakens.
>
> Now we understand why on our first meeting with him, the Friar spent so much time discussing the various plants he had picked. His expertise on their various properties convinces us that this may be the eventual means of Juliet's salvation. We know that things will go wrong and we think the drug may well be the cause of that. In fact, the plan will go wrong for a far simpler reason: lack of communication.

SCENE 2 – Wedding preparations

❶ The Capulets are organising the wedding.

❷ Juliet returns from Friar Lawrence to reveal to her delighted father that she will marry Paris.

❸ Capulet praises the part played by the Friar and heads off to tell Paris the good news.

❹ The marriage is brought forward to Wednesday.

CHECKPOINT 13

How have we been prepared for the Friar's ability to help the lovers?

GLOSSARY

vial small bottle used for medicines or poisons

Venus smiles not in a house of tears You cannot think of love when you are unhappy

CHECKPOINT 14

Who does Capulet want to conduct the marriage ceremony of Juliet and Paris?

The Capulets are preparing for the wedding when Juliet returns from the Friar. She is suitably apologetic for her earlier outburst and now asks for forgivenes from her father with an assurance that 'Henceforward I am ever ruled by you' (line 22).

Capulet's excitement that his heart is 'wondrous light' (line 46) at Juliet's change of heart is touching. His comment about the Friar that 'All our whole city is much bound to him' (line 32) is an ironic tribute. When Juliet has gone to bed, he is still as delighted as ever about the forthcoming wedding, prepared to stay up all night to make it a success.

The wedding moves closer

Things seem to be going to plan. The advance of the wedding by a further day speeds up the action even further.

SCENE 3 – Juliet takes the drug

1 Juliet is in her bedroom on the eve of the wedding ceremony.

2 She refuses her mother's request to let the Nurse stay with her.

3 Juliet describes her fears of waking in the tomb before Romeo arrives: she has horrid imaginings of the skeletons and corpses.

4 She drinks the potion and falls to her bed.

Juliet has retired to her room and has agreed on what she is to wear at the wedding. She wishes to be alone to put the plan into action.

Juliet's strength and courage are features of this scene. Her resourcefulness is evident in the opening exchanges with the Nurse and her mother where she skilfully arranges for each of them to leave her (lines 1–13).

A different Juliet appears when she is left on her own. The doubts she expresses about the Friar's true motives are interesting (lines 24–7).

They suggest a view of the Friar that is not entirely flattering and which might be felt to anticipate his actions in the closing moments of the play.

Juliet faces the grim task she has to perform with fortitude, in the full awareness of the horrors she may have to experience (lines 33–57). She ends the scene with the haunting words, 'Romeo, I come! this do I drink to thee' (line 58).

DID YOU KNOW?
Tchaikovsky used the play *Romeo and Juliet* for his 1870 Fantasy-ouverture.

Juliet's farewell

Juliet's soliloquy is in effect her farewell to the world. When she awakens in the tomb to discover Romeo lying dead beside her, there will be no time for a lengthy farewell. In fact, the scene she witnesses when she does regain consciousness is far worse than anything she has imagined. In her speech, she is more worried about what she will feel if she wakes before Romeo comes. Had she done so, the ending would have been happy.

SCENE 4 – The last-minute wedding preparations

1 At three o'clock in the morning of the wedding day, Capulet and his wife are already up making final preparations.

2 The Nurse is sent to rouse Juliet and 'trim her up' (line 24) as Capulet realises Paris has arrived.

This little scene provides a slight pause in the action. The Capulets are still rushing around making preparations for the wedding in the morning.

Last moments of normality

The family is preparing for Juliet's wedding, happily and excitedly. The irony is that the audience knows full well that upstairs Juliet is already rendering the preparations pointless.

GLOSSARY

wondrous light greatly cheered up

our whole city is much bound to him Verona owes him a great deal

trim her up get her dressed

EXAMINER'S SECRET

Keep an eye on the clock so you do not run out of time.

SCENE 5 – Juliet's body is discovered

❶ Unable to rouse Juliet, the Nurse discovers that the bride-to-be is apparently dead.

❷ Lord and Lady Capulet are overcome with grief.

❸ Friar Lawrence and Paris are the last to arrive at the grim scene.

❹ The family is engulfed in misery.

❺ The wedding is transformed into a funeral as Friar Lawrence takes charge of the burial arrangements.

CHECKPOINT 15

What suspicion about the Friar does Juliet express?

It falls to the Nurse to discover the dead Juliet and alert the rest of the family to the tragedy. The reactions of Juliet's parents to her death are rather too poetic though Capulet delivers a memorable couplet, 'Death lies on her like an untimely frost / Upon the sweetest flower of all the field' (lines 28–9). Finally the Friar and Paris arrive on a scene of utter grief as the Capulets and the Nurse loudly bewail their loss.

The Friar's speech (lines 65–83) contrasts sharply with the expressions of grief all round him. He reassures Capulet that he should not blame himself for Juliet's death since the 'most [he] sought was her promotion' (line 71). To those unaware of his part in Juliet's 'death', it would seem measured and reassuring; to the audience, it is obviously prepared.

Paris is given little to say but, when he speaks, he seems deeply upset by the loss of his beloved.

The scene ends with a curious interlude as the musicians discuss the new requirements now that the wedding has been changed for a funeral.

Reactions to Juliet's death

Some may feel that it is appropriate that the Nurse who has betrayed Juliet should be the one who has to break the dreadful news to the family. The response of the Capulets seems rather overdone but this allows the grief when it is for the real deaths to be far more meaningful.

CHECKPOINT 16

Why might the Capulets' response to Juliet's death be so poetic?

GLOSSARY

untimely frost a frosty spell that comes too early kills off the flowers

her promotion a better life for her

Now take a break!

WHO SAYS ...?

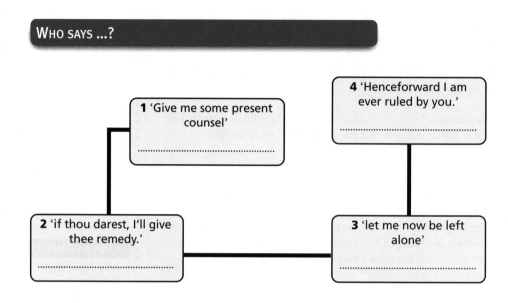

1 'Give me some present counsel'

....

4 'Henceforward I am ever ruled by you.'

....

2 'if thou darest, I'll give thee remedy.'

....

3 'let me now be left alone'

....

ABOUT WHOM?

5 'All our whole city is much bound to him.'

....

8 'Her blood is settled, and her joints are stiff.'

....

6 'See where she comes from shrift with merry look.'

....

7 'festering in his shroud'

....

Check your answers on p. 85.

SCENE 1 – Romeo in Mantua

① Romeo is in Mantua.

② Unaware of the true situation, Balthasar has come hotfoot from Verona to inform Romeo of Juliet's death.

③ Romeo resolves to return immediately to be with her.

④ He finds an apothecary who supplies him with a deadly poison.

Romeo is sad and alone in Mantua. His opening soliloquy recounts a dream that prefigures what is to happen in this scene. It is in this depressed state of mind that he greets Balthasar fresh from Verona.

> **CHECKPOINT 17**
>
> What are Romeo's options when he hears Balthasar's news?

His response to his friend's news, 'I defy you, stars!' (line 24), reminds the audience of the futility of what he intends to do. He is, after all, a 'star-crossed!' lover (I.Prologue.6). His hastiness in dismissing Balthasar is followed by an equally hasty visit to an apothecary he has already noticed in Mantua. Violently he demands poison from the unfortunate man for he is determined to 'lie with [Juliet] tonight' (line 34).

> **GLOSSARY**
> **I defy you, stars** Fate, do your worst

The Apothecary and the Friar

The description of the Apothecary (lines 37–54) is vaguely reminiscent of the Friar, and suggests parallels between the two men. The former has an expert understanding of drugs – Romeo had noticed him 'Culling of simples' (line 40) – which he can use to bring a swift death. The latter uses his powers to bring life. Ironically, Romeo uses the poison to gain everlasting life with Juliet. Even more ironic is the fact that the revenge Lady Capulet seeks on Romeo for killing Tybalt is identical: 'an unaccustomed dram'! (III.5.87–90)

SCENE 2 – The plan miscarries

❶ Friar John brings Friar Lawrence the letter to Romeo that has not been delivered.

❷ Lawrence dashes off to be with Juliet when she wakes from her drugged sleep.

Friar Lawrence is quite content that his plans are working. The arrival of Friar John, the carrier of the vital message to Romeo, alarms him; he realises the dangers he is running since 'The letter was not nice' (line 18). At this stage he is content since he thinks the non-delivery of the vital letter only affects Juliet. He sends Friar John an 'iron crow' (line 21) to open the Capulet vault so that he can keep Juliet at his cell until Romeo can be informed.

CHECKPOINT 18

What worries does Friar Lawrence have about Juliet?

Friar John's misfortune

The reasons for Friar John being unable to deliver the crucial letter would be laughable – he had been locked into a house where the plague was suspected – if the consequences were not so grave. The whole tragedy now hinges on a failure to deliver a letter, a trivial enough occurrence but one which reinforces the idea of Fate playing a hand in the lovers' untimely end.

SCENE 3 – The denouement

1 Paris is mounting a vigil over Juliet outside the Capulet family vault.

2 He hides when Romeo and Balthasar approach.

3 Having sent Balthasar away, Romeo proceeds to break down the door to the vault.

4 Paris steps forward to challenge Romeo. A bitter fight ensues which leads to the death of Paris.

5 Romeo lays Paris beside the dead body of Juliet.

6 He looks on her corpse, takes the poison and dies 'with a kiss' (line 120).

7 Friar Lawrence arrives in the vault and meets Balthasar as Juliet stirs.

8 The Friar hears the sounds of people approaching and tries unavailingly to persuade Juliet to leave the vault.

9 Frightened for his own safety, the Friar makes a hasty exit.

10 Juliet gazes at her dead husband. There is no poison left so she takes Romeo's dagger and stabs herself.

EXAMINER'S SECRET

In a typical examination essay you might use as many as eight quotations.

Events move to a rapid conclusion. Romeo dashes to the vault where he is confronted by Paris who is standing guard over Juliet's resting-place. The brief fight ends with Paris dead, in much the same way as earlier Romeo had despatched Tybalt in a flood of passion.

Paris's presence comes as a surprise but his grief is real and ultimately, even deservedly, it earns him a place beside Juliet.

Romeo, we know, is a ferocious fighter when his temper is up. Paris is destined to go the same way as Tybalt.

Now it is all a question of fatally-wrong timing: Romeo kills himself fractionally before Juliet awakens from her drugged sleep; the Friar is over-hasty in abandoning Juliet; and she kills herself before anyone can enter the vault.

GLOSSARY

Culling of simples picking herbs

an unaccustomed dram poison

not nice important

crow crowbar

Romeo's farewell speech to Juliet (lines 88–120) provides a beautiful conclusion to the love affair.

The Friar now realises that his entire plan has crumbled and he faces public disgrace. His suggestion that Juliet retires to a 'sisterhood of holy nuns' (line 157) seems remarkably cowardly. It removes her from public scrutiny but to a young woman who has just lost her husband it may not seem the ideal way to end one's days!

CHECKPOINT 19

Looking at the people on stage now, who would you blame for the deaths?

Soon the vault is crowded as the Prince, the Capulets and Lord Montague pour in to witness the tragedy. They contemplate the wretched scene, Montague announcing that his wife has died that very night of a broken heart. Friar Lawrence steps forward to describe the events that have led to this appalling situation.

The Friar is allowed a few words, though one might note that 'I will be brief' (line 229) introduces a speech that is thirty lines long!

The Prince accepts the explanation and reads the letter that Romeo had sent to his father. Turning to the surviving members of the feuding families, he condemns them for pursuing their quarrels. Capulet and Montague join hands and resolve to be friends by commemorating with statues the 'Poor sacrifices of our enmity' (line 304). As dawn approaches, the Prince delivers the final judgement on the love affair:

... never was a story of more woe
Than this of Juliet and her Romeo. (lines 309–10)

The play opens with a **sonnet**. It is fitting that it closes with one, shared by Capulet, Montague and the Prince (lines 297–310), with the last two lines completing both the **rhyming couplet** and the play.

The tragic ending

The lovers are fated to die, as we know from the opening lines of the play. Their deaths come across as the result of tragic mistakes, chiefly the result of people acting in haste. Romeo's rush of blood in III.1 leads to the death of Tybalt. Romeo reacts equally swiftly when he decides to return to Verona to be with Juliet. When challenged by Paris outside the vault, he does not hesitate but engages in a fight that leads to the death of Paris. The Friar has the chance to save Juliet at least, but hearing footsteps he panics and leaves her to her predictable suicide. Only at the end when five of Verona's finest young people have perished is there time to consider the consequences of what has occurred. At last common sense prevails when the Prince points out that 'All are punished' (line 295); and the 'parents' strife' (I.Prologue.8) is finally buried as the Prologue Act I had warned us.

CHECKPOINT 20

Who speaks the final words of the play?

GLOSSARY

sisterhood of holy nuns a nunnery

Poor sacrifices of our enmity the lovers who died because of their parents' hatred

Now take a break!

Test yourself (Act v)

Who says ...?

4 'I could not send it – here it is again'

....

1 'I dreamt my lady came and found me dead'

....

2 'Her body sleeps in Capel's monument'

....

3 'I sell thee poison: thou hast sold me none.'

....

About whom?

5 'Your looks are pale and wild'

....

8 'poor sacrifices of our enmity'

....

6 'Thy lips are warm.'

....

7 'Why art thou yet so fair?'

....

Check your answers on p. 85.

PART THREE

COMMENTARY

THEMES

LOVE

The play's enduring popularity stems from the fact that its subject matter is love and, for good measure, we are given at least four different variations on the theme.

Courtly love

Our first meeting with Romeo shows us a stylised conventional view of love, sometimes called courtly or **Petrarchan love**. This is what grips Romeo in the opening scenes of the play: he postures and sighs; he understands that Rosaline is not to be 'hit with Cupid's arrow' (I.1.206–7) yet neither is he able to forget her, nor despite the teasing of his friends, Benvolio and Mercutio, is he prepared to try and do so.

It is appropriate that his feelings, however ill-directed, should be so strong. He is adamant that no one but Rosaline will suit him, and it supplies a natural motive to go to the Capulets' masked ball. On the way to the ball (I.4) we are reminded of the power of his love for Rosaline, and of the misery it brings with it. He is confused by its illogical effect on him, 'Is love a tender thing? It is too rough, / Too rude, too boisterous, and it pricks like thorn.' (I.4.25–6) Moreover, he still has to endure Mercutio's gibes before he reaches his evening destination.

Sexual love

Yet, once at the ball, Romeo's first words (I.5.41) reveal the immediate impact that seeing Juliet has upon him. The effect Juliet has upon him is even more astonishing given his previous strength of feeling for Rosaline. However, to call this first emotion love is misleading: infatuation is surely a more apt description.

Another approach to love is presented in the opening scene, and throughout the play references are made to it. This might be called

EXAMINER'S SECRET
Always read the whole examination paper before you start writing.

sexual love. We first encounter it in the coarse humour of the servants in Act I, Scene 1. It crops up again in our first meeting with the Nurse when she jokes that 'Women grow by men' (I.3.93) and moments later is encouraging Juliet to view Paris sympathetically and 'seek happy nights to happy days' (I.3.103). Mercutio's conversations frequently employ lewd references that indicate a broad view of the relations between the sexes, though it has to be said that the use of **puns** adds a little delicacy to the humour.

Dutiful love

A third expression of love can be seen in Paris and his relationship – such as it is – with Juliet. This is characterised by the dutifulness of affection that attends an arranged marriage. It is interesting to note the Capulets' differing views of Paris. Initially Capulet is keen to protect his daughter and assures Paris that Juliet's decision is to be final in the matter. His wife, by contrast, is intent on the marriage right from the start: we can be quite sure that she herself was married young and quickly pregnant (I.3.69–71). The Nurse also approves of arranged marriages. Moreover, in the moment of Juliet's deepest despair, she counsels the expedient solution of arranged marriage with Paris as the way out of the dilemma.

CHECK THE FILM
West Side Story is a modern interpretation of *Romeo and Juliet*.

Although you might naturally resent the threat to Romeo and Juliet's happiness which is represented by Paris, you end up quite admiring the man for his constancy. He eventually perishes in the graveyard, fighting mistakenly to protect the dead from some sort of vengeful attack by Romeo. His 'love' is rewarded by earning him a place beside Juliet.

True love

The popularity of the play does not reside in its different definitions of love but in its triumphant description of one love. The 'true love' of Romeo and Juliet shines out against the other types of love. In the opening Chorus, they are described as 'star-crossed lovers' (I.Prologue.6) and on one level this suggests their love is fated. On another level, the choice of stars is appropriate to capture the luminous quality of their love. Elsewhere in these Notes there is reference to language (see **Language and style**) which will develop this point a little more securely, though here it is sufficient to observe throughout the text the way that the true love lights up the skies.

Romeo's first reaction to Juliet is that 'she doth teach the torches to burn bright' (I.5.44). When he catches sight of her in the orchard, she is the 'light [breaking] through yonder window' (II.2.2). Juliet shares this view of their love. Initially, she is suspicious of the suddenness of the feeling, fearing it is like lightning 'which doth cease to be / Ere one can say, "It lightens."' (II.2.119–20), yet by the wedding night she is making a comparison to the luminescent quality of Romeo's love:

> … when I shall die
> Take him and cut him out in little stars,
> And he will make the face of heaven so fine
> That all the world will be in love with night   (III.2.21–4)

CHECK THE NET

www. englishresources. co.uk for discussion topics

SOCIETY AT WAR

The tragic end of their love is a direct consequence of the other main theme in the play: a society at war with itself that makes their love at once so tragic and so beautiful. It is love against the odds. Romeo, we know from the very beginning of the play, has no business even to meet Juliet, a Capulet, let alone fall in love with her.

The masked ball is designed explicitly to cement an entirely different sort of love affair, yet into it comes an interloper whose magical encounter with a young woman totally rewrites the script. We are aware of the dangers all the time: the opening brawl, the bitterness of Tybalt, the perils of a Montague being discovered in the Capulet orchard, the street fighting in the heat of the summer. But against this background, a beautiful love forms, blossoms and achieves immortality.

It is the innocence and truth of this illicit love that has given the story its popularity across time. Each generation redefines its Shakespeare. Each generation suffers its own conflicts but, despite them, love, the finest expression of the human spirit, survives and thrives.

Love is used as a central theme in four of Shakespeare's **tragedies**: *Romeo and Juliet*, *Troilus and Cressida* (1602), *Othello* (1604) and

GLOSSARY

Women grow by men a reference to pregnancy .

Antony and Cleopatra (1607). It is tempting to see them in this order as describing love at four different ages, from the passion of the youngest lovers to the final search for love by Antony and Cleopatra, lovers who are again torn between two different worlds. Romeo and Juliet are, however, powerless in a world not of their making and one which they are unable to influence – at least not until they die.

DEATH

Romeo and Juliet die as a direct consequence of the hatreds of the society in which they find themselves. Their deaths make them permanent symbols of the power of love which triumphs through all adversity, one that is destined for ever to symbolise the wicked waste in all divided societies.

STRUCTURE

CHECK THE NET
For different ideas on staging the play look at
www.theatre. design.org.uk

The action of the story covers a period of five days: the opening street fight occurs on a Sunday morning and by early Thursday morning the lovers have died and the feuding families are united.

The plot revolves entirely around the lovers. We see them before they meet each other. We witness their first meeting. We follow them through their declarations of love and up to the crucial moment when Romeo kills Tybalt and all is lost. We sense them fighting against time as the wedding with Paris is brought forward and the Friar hatches his desperate scheme to save them.

Inevitably as events move so quickly, mistakes are made. The vital message fails to reach Romeo. Juliet rouses herself from her unconscious state fractionally too late to save Romeo and herself.

This concentration of time and action adds to the power of the story. The lovers are impelled unstoppably through a sequence of events and this adds to the feeling that they are caught up in a train of circumstances which is beyond their power to control.

It is the pace and urgency of the play that makes the drama so compelling. The plot is a complicated one only because we have to take so many factors into consideration to understand the complexities of the web in which Romeo and Juliet are entrapped. The absence of sub-plots ensures that throughout the 'two hours traffic' our attention is firmly fixed on the fate of the young lovers. (See Timeline.)

CHARACTERS

ROMEO

At the beginning of the play Romeo is conspicuously absent. We discover that he is suffering from lovesickness, the object of his unrequited devotions being Rosaline. He is adamant that there is no other woman for him, yet he is equally certain that Rosaline is not to be won by him. This accounts for the confusion that we see in his first conversation with Benvolio (I.1.158–236). His speech is characterised by **oxymoron** and contradictions as he struggles to make sense of his predicament.

His depression persists even when he is making his way to the ball to see Rosaline, and he is a soft target for Mercutio's wit though he feels that his low spirits proceed in some measure from a feeling that something dreadful will 'bitterly begin his fearful date' at the ball, something dreadful that will end with his 'untimely death' (I.4.109–12).

His confusion and self-doubt are immediately banished when he first sees Juliet and notices how she appears in the dance like a 'snowy dove trooping with crows' (I.5.48). There is some **irony** that this should be his reaction since he denied to Benvolio that he could possibly forget Rosaline in such a way. Within seconds, he takes Juliet's hand and their opening moments together are celebrated in a **sonnet**

By the time of the orchard scene (II.2), his transformation as a character is clear. He remains a gentle youth but now he has animation. He throws himself forward into the light to declare his love. Throughout the scene it is he who forces the pace and springs into action to arrange the marriage with Friar Lawrence. The Friar's conversation with him in Act II, Scene 3 confirms that Romeo has

EXAMINER'S SECRET
The answer booklet contains enough paper for you to get top marks!

Impetuous
Whole-hearted
Intense
Single-minded
Well-regarded

GLOSSARY
untimely premature

altered as a person: he is direct, offering no apologies for his
apparently inconsistent behaviour. 'Her I love now / Doth grace for
grace and love for love allow' (II.3.85).

By the time we see him next – in the company of his friends, Mercutio
and Benvolio – he is completely changed. Mercutio notices his
improved humour, 'Why, is not this better now than groaning for
love? / Now art thou sociable; now art thou Romeo' (II.4.86–7).

He even joins his friends in poking fun at the Nurse though he
displays the positive side of himself as he issues the instructions for
the wedding.

**CHECK
THE FILM**
Is Romeo presented
differently in the
films of *Romeo and
Juliet?*

His good humour is apparent after the wedding (III.1) when he joins
his friends on the hot streets of Verona. Tempers are rising in the heat
but not that of Romeo. He deliberately avoids confrontation with
Tybalt to the despair of Mercutio until he is drawn into the fight.
Mercutio's death he blames on his love for Juliet which 'hath made
(him) effeminate' (III.1.114). Impetuously he draws his sword and in
his rage quickly despatches Tybalt. Instantly he realises the
implications and utters the poignant words, 'O, I am fortune's fool'
(II.1.136).

Romeo in despair

Henceforth he loses his peace of mind. His conduct becomes ever
more erratic as he has lost what he has so fleetingly enjoyed. Now the
affected misery he had shown us in the opening scene is replaced by
genuine despair as he contemplates life without Juliet. He suffers from
uncontrollable grief before the Friar and the Nurse (III.3). He sees
banishment as 'torture and not mercy' (III.3.29) and draws his dagger
to commit suicide.

A poetic farewell

He enjoys one final exchange with Juliet sharing with her an aubade
in much the same way as he had shared a sonnet with her at the
beginning of their love. He takes his leave and when we meet him
again in Mantua his mood is brittle. His opening words show him in

fine spirits: he has dreamed that Juliet and he are to be reunited. His mood changes abruptly as he hears from Balthasar that Juliet's 'body sleeps in Capel's monument' (V.1.18). Impetuously he finds poison, terrifying the Apothecary into supplying him with it, and rushes back to Verona. Once there, nothing will stand in his way. He offers Paris the chance to escape. Paris dies like Tybalt before him, a victim of Romeo's rage. In a quieter mood he takes his final look at Juliet and swallows the poison.

Romeo is well regarded by the other characters. His mother expresses her relief that he has not taken part in the ugly street fight (I.1.115), whilst his father is concerned and baffled by his apparent depression. Benvolio cares for him enough to pursue the matter and to take the problem seriously. Mercutio is another who seeks to cheer him up. When Tybalt is offering to do violence to Romeo, it is Capulet who springs to his defence, 'Verona brags of him / To be a virtuous and well-governed youth' (I.5.67–8).

JULIET

Juliet's youth is a key factor in forming a view of her character. She is innocent and young, not quite fourteen years of age. Her father is keen to protect her since she is his only surviving child. When her mother broaches the question of marriage, Juliet avoids a direct answer, 'It is an honour that I dream not of' (I.3.64). She consents to consider Paris but promises to make no commitment without her mother's approval (I.3.95–7).

When she meets Romeo, she is no longer passive. At first she allows Romeo to kiss her (I.5.105) but she encourages him to kiss her again (I.5.108) and compliments him into the bargain, 'You kiss by the book' (I.5.110). By the end of the scene as she endeavours to discover the identity of this stranger, we note the charming indirectness of manner as she includes Romeo as one of three men whose names she wants (I.5.128–34). Her next response to the Nurse shows how already she is beginning to hide her feelings as she describes her dismay at realising Romeo's family connections as 'a rhyme I learnt' (I.5.142).

- Young
- Sensitive
- Vulnerable
- Resourceful
- Courageous

GLOSSARY

effeminate afraid to fight

fortune's fool a pawn of fate

monument family vault

**CHECK
THE FILM**
Gwyneth Paltrow
won an Oscar for
Best Actress 1998 as
Juliet in
*Shakespeare in
Love.*

Juliet's confusion

In the Balcony scene, Juliet is anxious to establish that she is not an immodest girl. She is embarrassed that she has betrayed her 'true-love passion' (II.2.104) so openly. There follows a spirited exchange which culminates in her proposal of marriage (II.2.142–8). Thereafter, her excitement is revealed in her confusion, forgetfulness and delay in departure.

Her wholehearted love is plain by the time the Nurse returns with Romeo's arrangements (II.5). Her serious-mindedness makes her an easy target for the Nurse's teasing.

Juliet is deserted

By the time we see her again she is awaiting Romeo on her wedding night (III.2). There is little doubt that she is eagerly anticipating the physical consummation of their marriage. She describes herself as an 'impatient child that hath new robes / And may not wear them' (III.2.30–1). She plunges from high excitement to the depths of misery as she contemplates life without her Romeo. The Nurse fetches him and they enjoy a single night before we see them preparing to part. She is left with one friend, the Nurse, with whom she can be honest. She soon loses even that comfort as the Nurse advises that she take Paris (III.5.212–25).

The strength of love

Isolated, Juliet turns to the Friar for a solution. Her cleverness with words is seen in her brief exchange with Paris (IV.1.18–43), then she pours out her despair to Friar Lawrence. The plan he expounds demands real courage and she derives it from her love. 'Love give me strength! and strength shall help afford', she cries at the end of the scene (IV.1.125).

To ensure the smooth operation of the plan, she summons up reserves of resource that indicate her growing maturity. She convinces her parents that she has changed her mind and is ready to marry Paris (IV.2.15–37). Then she hides her feelings from the Nurse, her one-time confidante, and her mother to give her the solitude she now needs. It is a 'dismal scene [she] needs must act alone' (IV.3.19). Her final speech (IV.3.20–58) shows her courage and strength of purpose as she contemplates the horrors she may face.

When she awakes in the vault, we can be absolutely certain that she will choose to die beside her Romeo, so completely has she embraced his love.

MERCUTIO

A convenient way to understand Mercutio is to consider his name (see **characternym**). A mercurial person is eloquent, active, sprightly and changeable – attributes that are certainly evident in Mercutio.

Mercutio is an attractive character who brings life and fun into the play. He is not involved in the opening street fight and we first meet him accompanying Romeo to the Capulets' ball. He is very different from the serious-minded Benvolio. His blunt advice to Romeo is to be 'rough with love' (I.4.27) and he tries to rouse Romeo out of his depression through enjoyment.

His earthy sense of humour emerges when he looks for Romeo after the Capulets' ball. The jests seem inappropriate here since events have moved on and Rosaline is an irrelevance. Later when he and Benvolio are discussing Tybalt's challenge to Romeo, he expresses a doubt that the lovesick Romeo has the strength to take on Tybalt. **Ironically**, after his death Romeo utters similar sentiments, 'Thy beauty hath … softened valour's steel' (III.1.114–5). Mercutio's affection for Romeo is clear in the witty interchange before the Nurse arrives with Juliet's message (II.4.37–97).

Gregarious
Lively
Witty
Loyal
Daring

We are to meet him for a final time at the opening of Act III. He berates Benvolio for suggesting they avoid trouble, and refuses to leave when Tybalt enters. We are already aware of the contempt in which he holds the man whom he considers merely a 'courageous captain of compliments' (II.4.20–1) so we sense his mounting rage as Romeo declines to duel with Tybalt. Finally he can bear this 'vile submission' (III.1.72) no longer and draws his sword on the 'rat-catcher' (III.1.74).

> **GLOSSARY**
> rat-catcher another reference to 'Cat', Tybalt's nickname, as cats were sometimes called 'Tyb'

He is fatally wounded as his friend intervenes to protect him.

Characteristically, his immediate response is to make light of the injury (III.4.95–101) but hearing Romeo's lame excuse, he realises the gravity of the wound and utters the cry that for ever sums up the fate of the innocent, 'A plague o' both your houses!' (III.1.106).

It has been suggested that Shakespeare kills off Mercutio because he is such an attractive character but it is his death that is the turning-point of the play. His affection means so much to Romeo that we know he cannot help but seek vengeance. Up to the moment of Mercutio's death, the play might have been a **comedy**. Now, a tragic conclusion is inevitable.

THE NURSE

The Nurse is Juliet's closest friend and confidante at the outset of the play. This is hardly surprising since she has been Juliet's wet-nurse. She is not, however, a particularly clever or sensitive woman and in the early part of the play she comes across as a comic figure. Certainly she provides considerable amusement in Act I, Scene 3 when Lady Capulet is discussing the possibility of marriage to Paris.

Whilst the mother treats the proposal with a degree of strained delicacy, the Nurse offers a far more down-to-earth interpretation of what young men can do for young women! Interestingly, she knows precisely how young Juliet is but makes no effort to suggest that this is a problem.

When Juliet falls for Romeo and asks the Nurse to discover his identity (I.5.128), it is significant that she is not drawn into Juliet's confidence: this appears to be the first time Juliet has concealed any secrets from her. Nevertheless, the Nurse relishes the role of go-between that Juliet asks of her. She is quick to warn Romeo not to lead Juliet into a 'fool's paradise' (II.4.160–61), particularly because 'the gentlewoman is young' (II.4.162). One suspects that she likes men; she is clearly taken with Romeo.

On her return with Romeo's good news, she enjoys the power the knowledge has given her as she evades Juliet's urgent questions (II.5. 25–64).When we meet her again, she is bringing Juliet the shocking news of Tybalt's death. By now she has turned against Romeo and is

Talkative
Scatter-brained
Compassionate
Fun-loving
Insecure

convinced that Juliet must share her feelings. 'Will you speak well of him that killed your cousin?' (III.2.96) is her incredulous reaction.

Betrayal of Juliet

The force of Juliet's grief persuades her to render a final act of assistance by fetching Romeo from the Friar's cell. When the lovers part, she and the Capulets come to Juliet's room to inform her that the marriage with Paris has been brought forward. She offers a token defence of Juliet but is quickly crushed by Capulet with 'Peace, you mumbling fool!' (III.5.172). Now she rapidly changes sides, praising Paris as 'a lovely gentleman!' (III.5.218). She has forfeited any closeness with Juliet. Her last duty in the play is to be the one who discovers the supposedly dead Juliet. Her grief is piercing but it seems a fair price to pay for her betrayal.

FRIAR LAWRENCE

The Friar's role in the play parallels that of the Nurse. He is respected by Romeo and is genuinely fond of the young man. He examines Romeo's reasons for abandoning Rosaline in favour of Juliet with some rigour, and is quick to point out the inconsistencies of behaviour. Nevertheless he is persuaded that what Romeo had felt for Rosaline was not love but love 'read by rote that could not spell' (II.3.88).

He has what may be called a sense of destiny: he feels it is in his power to alter the course of history, which impels him to agree to conduct the marriage ceremony in the hopes that it might 'turn your households' rancour to pure love' (II.3.92). He is right, though not in the way that he had anticipated. Despite his prophetic reservation that 'These violent delights have violent ends' (II.6.9), he unites the pair in marriage.

Pompous,
Self-important
Dependable ... but
only to a point!
Unworldly

His plan to reconcile the families, however, soon comes to grief. He is left to break the news of the Prince's judgement to Romeo. He is taken aback by the force of Romeo's emotions and looks for a different solution. Romeo is to go to Mantua where he can live until the time is ripe 'To blaze your marriage, reconcile your friends, / Beg pardon of the Prince, and call thee back' (III.3.150-51). This second plan is as unsteady as the first.

He is now deeply enmired in the **tragedy** and when Juliet comes to him for assistance in Act IV, Scene 1, he comes up with a third plan which is even more far-fetched than the previous two. We already know that he is some kind of a herbalist from his first appearance and he draws on this knowledge to extricate Juliet from the deep trouble she now faces. The cynical might wonder if the Friar might at this stage be thinking as much about his own skin as that of Juliet. Certainly the thought crosses Juliet's mind, as she prepares to take the potion, wondering if he has poisoned her 'Lest ... he should be dishonoured / Because he married me before to Romeo?' (IV.3.26–7).

The plan goes wrong when the message to Romeo in Mantua is not delivered. He hurries to the Capulets' vault to be with the waking Juliet. He tries in vain to persuade Juliet to leave the dead Romeo and escape with him. When she refuses, he deserts her. Eventually he comes forward to reveal the truth. We might have expected that some dire punishment will follow but the Prince excuses him with 'We still have known thee for a holy man' (V.3.270). It is a rather gentle rebuke: yet Friar Lawrence's real punishment is that he has to live with the consequences of his own actions for the rest of his life.

BENVOLIO

As with Mercutio, there is some advantage in considering the derivation of Benvolio's name. It comes loosely from two Latin words which may be translated as 'I wish (or mean) well'. His first line, 'Part, fools!' (I.1.61) casts him as a sensible peacemaker, a role he plays throughout the play.

Benvolio is a close and sensitive friend to Romeo able to judge 'his affections by my own' (I.1.124). His response to Romeo's dilemma over Rosaline is sympathetic yet practical, 'forget to think of her ... / By giving liberty unto thine eyes' (I.1.223–5). Moreover, this advice is precisely what does happen.

Well-meaning
Sensible
Sensitive

His various conversations with Mercutio throw into sharper relief his essential niceness. He is not drawn into coarse comment and violent reaction. In fact, when Mercutio and Romeo are indulging in some explicit sexual jesting, he draws it to a halt with a 'Stop there, stop there' (II.4.92).

He realises the potential dangers of the summer heat and tries to dissuade Mercutio from risking another street brawl. When he fails, he is the one who urges Romeo to leave the scene, knowing the likely reaction of the Prince. It falls to him in a speech reminiscent of his description of the first brawl (I.1.104–113) to relate to the Prince the events that have resulted in the deaths of Mercutio and Tybalt. Despite Lady Capulet's allegation of bias, 'He is a kinsman to the Montague' (III.1.176), his version is accepted, a factor which goes some way to alleviating the sentence on Romeo.

Benvolio's contribution to the drama ends here. The story moves on without him. In a sense this is fitting. He represents good sense and tolerance, qualities that are swallowed up in the bitterness that follows the deaths of Mercutio and Tybalt.

TYBALT

In contrast to Mercutio and Benvolio, Tybalt is a relatively one-dimensional character. Nonetheless, Mercutio mistakes the true Tybalt when he describes him as belonging to the fashionable set of 'lisping, affecting fantasticoes' (II.4.29), for Tybalt is a dangerous man.

Tybalt appears first when Benvolio is endeavouring to separate the warring factions in Act I, Scene 1. He goes for his sword, rejecting Benvolio's plea to 'keep the peace' (I.1.65). His response sums up all you need to know about his part in the play: 'What, drawn, and talk of peace! I hate the word / As I hate hell, all Montagues and thee' (I.1.67–8).

He is obliged to withdraw by the entry and strong words of the Prince but his seething hatred of all things Montague is not eased. When he overhears Romeo at the masked ball, he again looks for his sword. '… by the stock and honour of my kin, / To strike him dead, I hold it not a sin' (I.5.58–9). Once more his rage is blunted, and once more he is forced to withdraw.

His third and final appearance in Act III, Scene 1 sees him in typically aggressive mood. He has sent a challenge to Romeo and is happy enough to take on Mercutio even before Romeo comes on. He

- Hot-tempered
- Vindictive
- Aggressive

GLOSSARY

fantasticoes
derogatory term for 'dandies'

EXAMINER'S SECRET

Plan your answers – then you will not repeat yourself.

brushes aside Romeo's attempts at friendliness, needling Romeo until Mercutio steps in. He takes to his heels when Mercutio falls, yet returns for one last time unconcerned by the news of Mercutio's death and happy to send Romeo to join him.

Tybalt represents the ugliness that lies just below the surface in this divided society. It is interesting to contrast the consequences of his death with those of Romeo and Juliet. His death ensures that more deaths will follow; the lovers' deaths that the killing comes to an end. If Verona is a divided society, Tybalt is the one man who wishes it to remain so.

LORD CAPULET

Lord Capulet's first appearance, bustling in wearing a night-shirt and calling for a sword to join the fight (I.1.72), might suggest he is a comic figure, especially since his wife remarks he would be better off with a crutch (I.1.73). Such a verdict is misleading. We next encounter him discussing with Paris an arranged marriage (I.2). Here we note his affectionate and protective attitude towards his daughter: she is young, a 'stranger in the world' (I.2.8) but above all she is 'the hopeful lady of my earth' (I.2.15). He offers Paris his support but 'My will to her consent is but a part' (I.2.17).

We view his acceptance of Romeo's presence at the masked ball as an act of kindness. We have already met Tybalt and it is a relief to see his kinsman standing up to his anger. Capulet comes across as a well-meaning, generous-spirited person. The death of Tybalt changes that. It is tempting to read into Capulet's change of heart a sense of responsibility for the tragic events in the second street fight (III.1) because his attitude towards Juliet is dramatically altered. He tells Paris 'I think she will be ruled / In all respects by me', adding ominously 'nay, more, I doubt it not' (III.4.13–14). Gone now is his tolerance towards Juliet. He rages at her when she refuses to marry Paris, then threatens to cast her out of the house when she persists.

In the closing moments of the play he rediscovers the kindliness we have seen in him at the beginning of the play. He it is who makes the first move, 'O brother Montague, give me thy hand' (V.3.296). For the sake of the drama, Capulet must behave dictatorially with Juliet; otherwise she would not have felt obliged to go to such lengths to conceal her marriage. Underneath, however, we feel that Capulet is a kindly man who suffers from the prejudice of his times.

PRINCE ESCALUS

Like other characters, the Prince is a victim of circumstances. He is always just too late to do anything other than react. He is plainly angered by the families' feud yet lacks the strength to reconcile their differences. After the first street fight, he threatens the severest punishment if the fighting does not stop.

Summoned to the scene of a double murder, he has the opportunity to enforce the death penalty on Romeo. On the one hand he claims that 'Mercy but murders, pardoning those that kill' (III.1.197), suggesting kindness is no deterrent, yet he is content to exile Romeo in a paradoxical act of kindness. It is left to him at the close of the play to sum up the consequences of the families' bitter conflict. He accepts some responsibility for what has happened by 'winking at [their] discords' (V.3.294). He can, however, claim some credit for forcing the two sides together by reminding them, 'what a scourge is laid upon your hate, / That heaven finds means to kill your joys with love' (V.3.292–3).

PARIS

Paris eventually lies in death beside Juliet. This he deserves. He pursues his love for Juliet quite single-mindedly but sensitively. His opening lines indicate his regrets about the feud between the Montagues and Capulets: 'Of honourable reckoning are you both, / And pity 't is you lived at odds so long' (I.2.4–5).

He accepts Capulet's advice about seeking Juliet's affections, and throughout the play treats her with respect and dignity. Seen from his point of view, it is absolutely right to prevent Romeo whom, he supposes, is responsible for Juliet's death, from doing 'some villainous shame / To the dead bodies' (V.3.52–3) and he dies defending her. Characteristically, his last thoughts are of her, 'lay me with Juliet' (V.3.73).

GLOSSARY
My will to her consent is but a part I will do what she wants
winking ignoring

His love for Juliet resembles that expressed by Romeo for Rosaline
except that he dies for it.

LANGUAGE AND STYLE

There is considerable variety of language use in Romeo and Juliet. By
and large, as in other Shakespearean plays, the nobility speak in **blank
verse**, whilst the lower classes employ **prose**. A clear illustration of
this can be seen in the opening scene of the play where the servants
exchange insults in prose, but this gives way to blank verse when the
more aristocratic members of the cast deliver their lines.

Blank verse was first used by Henry Howard, Earl of Surrey, in the
middle of the sixteenth century. Much of the finest poetry verse – by
Shakespeare, Milton, Tennyson and Wordsworth – has been in this
form. It can also be found in German and Italian drama. Its strength
lies in its ability to capture the natural rhythms of speech.

The term does not mean unrhymed poetry. Technically, **blank verse**
consists of unrhymed **iambic pentameters**: in other words a line with
ten syllables, five of which are stressed as indicated in this line:

'Who nów the príce of hís dear blóod doth ówe?'

Shakespeare's blank verse uses this basic pattern but he is never tied
down: he captures the sound of speech with a range of strategies to
vary the length and rhythm of lines. The famous speech of Juliet (II.2)
provides some interesting examples that a higher-grade student might
comment upon:

Juliet: What's in a name? That which we call a rose
            By any other word would smell as sweet.
            So Romeo would, were he not Romeo called,
            Retain that dear perfection which he owes
            Without that title. Romeo, doff thy name,
            And for that name, which is no part of thee,
            Take all myself.

Romeo: (*To Juliet*) I take thee at thy word.   (II.2.43–9)

In these lines, Juliet is wondering why Romeo's family name alone makes him an unsuitable man to love. Shakespeare uses the soliloquy to enable her to think out loud and reveal her deepest feelings. Say this speech aloud, using the punctuation marks to help your phrasing, and you will notice that it has something of the feeling of a person wrestling with ideas.

Look at those punctuation marks again and you will notice lines that are not end-stopped, that is they do not have punctuation marks at the end of them. The effect of this is to break up the rhythm which blank verse imposes. This is a poetic technique known as enjambement. There are also a couple of occasions where the sentence ends in the middle of a line. This too breaks up the rhythm, and reinforces the idea of a person struggling to come to terms with ideas. It may come as a surprise but there is a name for this deliberate breaking of a line of poetry: caesura

Finally, observe that Juliet finishes her speech, 'Take all myself.' in the middle of the line of blank verse. And Romeo chimes in to complete the line, picking up the word, 'take', and accepting her offer. It is as though Juliet has started the line and the thought, and Romeo, acting in harmony, completes both the line and the thought.

It is his genius for using poetic forms to support and deepen emotion that makes Shakespeare a truly great writer.

Shakespeare also uses the blank verse rhythm – the iambic pentameter – with rhyme. When the rhymes are paired, they are known as rhyming couplets. It is a fact that in his earlier plays, Shakespeare used a higher percentage of rhymed lines. As he grew older, he seems to have realised that blank verse was far more flexible for his purposes.

One place where the rhymed couplet is used regularly is at the end of a scene or act. This has the effect of neatly rounding off the action. Look at the last two lines of the play, where the rhythm of the lines combined with the final rhyme signal to the audience that the end has come – and it's time for the applause! Another use of the rhymed couplet at the end of a scene might be to warn the actors waiting in the wings that it is time to enter.

EXAMINER'S SECRET
If you are asked to make a comparison, use comparing words such as, 'on the other hand', 'however' and 'by contrast'.

DID YOU KNOW?

There are at least 175 puns in this play.

The language at times seems rather overloaded with linguistic tricks – puns, antitheses, paradoxes and oxymoron. In part this may be explained by the influence of **Petrarch** and his love poetry. It is also the case that Shakespeare always enjoyed playing around with words, even when it seems inappropriate!

The basis of **figurative language** is the comparison. At its simplest, you can compare something directly with something else: '... she hangs upon the cheek of night / As a rich jewel in an Ethiop's ear' (I.5.45–6). This sort of direct comparison is known as a **simile**

A more subtle form of comparison is the **metaphor**. There are numerous examples but Romeo uses it particularly effectively when he sees Juliet on her balcony (II.2.2): 'What light through yonder window breaks? / It is the east, and Juliet is the sun'

Similes and metaphors form part of the play's **imagery**. The continual references to sources of bright light, lightning itself, gunpowder and explosions affect the audience's imaginative responses. Romeo and Juliet are 'star-crossed lovers' (I.Prologue.6). On one level the stars represent fate – the pair are fated to die. On another level a star may be seen as something bright which shows up against the darkness of the night sky. What we have is a love which is brilliant but short-lived, passing across the dark face of a troubled society. Additionally, the image carries with it excitement and a compelling speed of action.

Once you start looking for references to their love being seen as a light for the world, you will probably be amazed at how often they occur. Look at Juliet's speech when she is anxiously awaiting the arrival of Romeo on their wedding night. She wants him so much but even at this moment of sheer joy, she anticipates his death. Notice the words she uses which convey how she sees him: '... when I shall die , / Take him and cut him out in little stars' (III.2.21–2).

One final point on the language of the play is the variety of poetic forms that Shakespeare employs. As is noted elsewhere, he employs the **sonnet** form on a number of occasions: most obviously in the opening Chorus to Acts I and II, and, more subtly, to elevate the opening lines of Romeo and Juliet's love affair (I.5.93–106).

The point about the sonnet is that it has a strict form with an intricate rhyming scheme. Shakepeare's sonnets employ a common pattern. If you call the first rhyme A, the second B, and so on, you can represent the rhyming scheme in this way:

DID YOU KNOW?
Shakespeare wrote 154 sonnets.

ABAB CDCD EFEF GG

There are three verses of four lines – or **quatrains** – and a final rhyming couplet. When you look more closely at the **sonnet** where the lovers meet for the first time (I.5.93–106), you will see that the first quatrain is given to Romeo, the second to Juliet. The lovers share the next four lines and between them they compose the final couplet. What makes the poetry so effective is that it is as if each is instantly on each other's wavelength. A sure sign that they are in love!

Throughout the play the poetry is often quite deliberately employed, sometimes a little too artificially in the circumstances: the Capulets, the Nurse and Paris grieving for the 'dead' Juliet is a notable example (IV.5.14–64).

The higher-grade candidate goes beyond the story-line to consider the way Shakespeare uses his poetic genius to create a language – which in all its diversity can capture the most beautiful love story of all time.

EXAMINER'S SECRET
An A-grade candidate can analyse a variety of the writer's techniques.

Now take a break!

PART FOUR

RESOURCES

HOW TO USE QUOTATIONS

One of the secrets of success in writing essays is the way you use quotations. There are five basic principles:

EXAMINER'S SECRET

Short, snappy quotations are always the best.

❶ Put inverted commas at the beginning and end of the quotation.

❷ Write the quotation exactly as it appears in the original.

❸ Do not use a quotation that repeats what you have just written.

❹ Use the quotation so that it fits into your sentence.

❺ Keep the quotation as short as possible.

Quotations should be used to develop the line of thought in your essays. Your comment should not duplicate what is in your quotation. For example:

Prince Escalus says that the families have caused public brawls three times before:
'Three civil brawls bred of an airy word ...
Have thrice disturbed the quiet of our streets'   (I.1.87–9)

Far more effective is to write:

The Prince condemns the families for having 'Three civil brawls'

Always lay out the lines as they appear in the text. For example:

Lady Capulet tells her daughter that she is not too young to marry since:
'Here in Verona, ladies of esteem,
Are made already mothers.'   (I.3.68–9)

or

'Here in Verona, ladies of esteem / Are made already mothers.'
(I.3.68–9)

However, the most sophisticated way of using the writer's words is to embed them into your sentence:

Mercutio is pleased to see a new more 'sociable' Romeo after the masked ball.

When you use quotations in this way, you are demonstrating the ability to use text as evidence to support your ideas – not simply including words from the original to prove you have read it.

CHECK THE NET

www.atschool. eduweb.co.uk for some interesting projects combining information technology

COURSEWORK ESSAY

Set aside an hour or so at the start of your work to plan what you have to do.

● List all the points you feel are needed to cover the task. Collect page references of information and quotations that will support what you have to say. A helpful tool is the highlighter pen: this saves painstaking copying and enables you to target precisely what you want to use.

● Focus on what you consider to be the main points of the essay. Try to sum up your argument in a single sentence, which could be the closing sentence of your essay. Depending on the essay title, it could be a statement about a character: In the final analysis the Friar is a coward: at the moment when Juliet needs him most as she awakens in the vault, he saves his own skin; an opinion about setting: The divisions of Verona are to be found even today in civil wars; or a judgement on a theme: I think the theme of *Romeo and Juliet* – headstrong youth against society's prejudices – is to be found in every period of history.

● Make a short essay plan. Use the first paragraph to introduce the argument you wish to make. In the following paragraphs develop this argument with details, examples and other possible points of view. Sum up your argument in the last paragraph. Check you have answered the question.

● Write the essay, remembering all the time the central point you are making.

EXAMINER'S SECRET

Higher level achievement begins at the point when you show you are aware of being marked.

- On completion, go back over what you have written to eliminate careless errors and improve expression. Read it aloud to yourself, or, if you are feeling more confident, to a relative or friend.

If you can, try to type your essay using a word processor. This will allow you to correct and improve your writing without spoiling its appearance.

SITTING THE EXAMINATION

Examination papers are carefully designed to give you the opportunity to do your best. Follow these handy hints for exam success:

BEFORE YOU START

EXAMINER'S SECRET

Read all parts of the question carefully to make sure your answer is complete.

- Make sure you know the subject of the examination so that you are properly prepared and equipped.

- You need to be comfortable and free from distractions. Inform the invigilator if anything is off-putting, e.g. a shaky desk.

- Read the instructions, or rubric, on the front of the examination paper. You should know by now what you have to do but check to reassure yourself.

- Observe the time allocation – and follow it carefully. If they recommend 60 minutes for Question 1 and 30 minutes for Question 2, it is because Question 1 carries twice as many marks.

- Consider the mark allocation. You should write a longer response for 4 marks than for 2 marks.

WRITING YOUR RESPONSES

- Use the questions to structure your response, e.g. question: 'The endings of X's poems are always particularly significant. Explain their importance with reference to two poems.' The first part of your answer will describe the ending of the first poem; the second part will look at the ending of the second poem; the third part will be an explanation of the significance of the two endings.

- Write a brief draft outline of your response.

- A typical 30-minute examination essay is probably between 400 and 600 words in length.

- Keep your writing legible and easy to read, using paragraphs to show the structure of your answers.

- Spend a couple of minutes afterwards quickly checking for obvious errors.

WHEN YOU HAVE FINISHED

- Don't be downhearted – if you found the examination difficult, it is probably because you really worked at the questions. Let's face it, they are not meant to be easy!

- Don't pay too much attention to what your friends have to say about the paper. Everyone's experience is different and no two people ever give the same answers.

IMPROVE YOUR GRADE

Your potential grades in any examination can be improved. An examiner marks your work according to a mark scheme that is applied to all candidates and no examiner knows in advance your level of achievement. Thus every candidate everywhere starts at the same point: a blank answer booklet.

The exam board has determined that your answer booklet has more than enough space in it for you to get the highest marks so there's no need to rush your writing to fill up three or four extra sheets! Moreover, the two hours your examination is scheduled to last will be enough for a candidate to secure the highest marks without rushing.

So take your time. Think carefully, plan carefully, write carefully and check carefully. A relaxed performer always works best – in any field and in every examination! Whatever you are studying, the way to be completely at ease with it in an examination is to know it inside out. There is no substitute for reading and re-reading the text.

EXAMINER'S SECRET
Beware of feeling you have to finish an answer because you have reached the bottom of the page.

DID YOU KNOW?
Shakespeare did not write essays!

Romeo and Juliet is conveniently divided into five acts and in your study strategy you should make use of these divisions. Using a single sheet for each act and list what happens in the story. This enables you to be familiar with the precise sequence of events.

Do the same for characters, devoting a single sheet to each of them. On this you should identify who they are, what they do and what they say. Back up the notes with short relevant quotations. These can be used to build up a character study or to support comments you wish to make in an essay.

You may be allowed to take the text into the examination hall but reference to it may well cost you valuable time unless you know it thoroughly. Your revision notes on plot and character are the ideal last-minute revision aids. You will almost certainly know more than enough to secure a high grade; the important thing is to make the most of what you have learnt.

The main reason why candidates let themselves down in the examination room is that they *fail to read the question*! Do not begin writing until you are quite sure what you want to say because it is very easy to lose track and end up writing off the subject. Whilst you are writing, it is a good idea to check back occasionally to the question and satisfy yourself that you are still answering it.

Keep an eye on the clock. Most literature papers require you to answer two questions in two hours. It may seem obvious but it is worth reminding yourself that to do yourself justice you need to spend about an hour on each question! This is all the more important when you feel happier answering one question rather than the other. If you steal time to produce a lengthy answer on one question, you are far more likely to lose all the extra marks you have gained by handing in a feeble response for the question you did not like.

Read the notes given below that describe the qualities that examiners are looking for in different quality responses and apply them to your work.

IMPROVING YOUR RESPONSE FROM A D TO A C

- Instead of writing, 'Romeo's love for Rosaline is quickly forgotten', you would write, 'Romeo goes to the ball with the clear intention of seeing Rosaline. When he sees Juliet, he is immediately swept off his feet by her beauty and he says, "I ne'er saw true beauty till this night" (I.5.53). All thoughts of Rosaline disappear.'

- Instead of putting in a number of quotations to show how struck he is by Juliet's beauty, note that he says, 'Did my heart love till now?' (I.5.52), and contrast that with his feelings for Rosaline when he tells Benvolio, 'This love feel I, that felt no love in this' (I.1.180).

- Instead of noting that the writer compares Juliet with a 'snowy dove trooping with crows' (I.5.48) you could comment that he uses a metaphor that vividly brings out the difference between Juliet and other girls.

The key difference between a D candidate and a C candidate is greater attention to the details that support your argument. The C candidate is aware of the examiner, is concerned with doing more than re-telling the story, and uses quotations to give substance to his/her writing.

EXAMINER'S SECRET
Everything you write on your answer sheet is marked.

IMPROVING YOUR RESPONSE FROM A C TO A B

- Instead of writing that he falls instantly in love with Juliet because of her beauty, you could note the various images which refer to her bringing light into his life: Juliet 'teaches the torches to shine bright' (I.5.44).

- Instead of putting in a couple of quotations, use detail from the whole text that collectively create a sense of his being blinded by her beauty: she is hanging like a rich ear-ring 'upon the cheek of night' (I.5.45).

- Instead of commenting that the writer uses similes or metaphors, you could indicate that he uses a range of poetic techniques to create an effect and give examples.

The key difference between a C and a B candidate is the awareness that a writer uses a range of techniques in order to convey ideas more effectively to the audience. The B candidate is beginning to explore

EXAMINER'S SECRET

You are always given credit for writing your essay plans.

his/her responses with a range of examples that pick out Shakespeare's deliberate attempts to convey ideas through words.

IMPROVING YOUR RESPONSE FROM A B TO AN A

- Instead of just observing how the Romeo feels, you can show how you share his views and can empathise with his ideas; for example, the sense of being bowled over by your first encounter with someone who is irresistibly attractive.

- Instead of just using references to illustrate the nature of love at first sight, you now present a line of thought about the poem with quotations to secure your argument.

- Instead of observing the poetic techniques used by the poet, you start to analyse how the thoughts and feelings are enhanced by the poet's use of language. Romeo's use of language changes when he falls in love with Juliet, and their first meeting is expressed in a sonnet.

The key difference between a B candidate and an A candidate is a sense that the audience can identify with the concerns of the characters and analyse how it is that the writer has succeeded in creating this work of art. The A candidate succeeds in going beneath the surface of the play and is able to see how Shakespeare works to achieve his effects. Romeo and Juliet are 'star-crossed lovers' (I.Prologue.6) at different levels. On a simple level, failure is written into their stars or fate, and they are doomed from the very outset of the play. On a more sophisticated level, they are 'star-crossed lovers' in the sense that the brilliance of their love stands out in the darkness of the society in which they live.

EXAMINER'S SECRET

The best candidates give their own interpretations of the text.

When you have finished, take a final look through what you have written. This is not a very enjoyable experience – for any of us who have taken examinations – but it is a necessary process. You may have made any number of silly errors under the pressure of exam conditions so use your last chance to make your answer the best it can be.

Once your examination is over you can look forward to the long summer holidays with the prospect of good news when the results are published in late August. Good luck!

SAMPLE ESSAY PLAN

A typical essay question on *Romeo and Juliet* is followed by a sample
essay plan in note form. This does not present the only answer to the
question, merely one answer. Do not be afraid to include your own
ideas and leave out some of the ones in this sample! Remember that
quotations are essential to prove and illustrate the points you make.

> To what extent is Friar Lawrence responsible for the deaths of
> Romeo and Juliet?

Such a question is anticipating quite a wide-ranging response. You
may feel that the Friar might bear considerable responsibility for the
lovers' untimely ending but in order to respond to that most nebulous
of examination question wordings, 'to what extent', you have to put
his role in context.

PART 1

Description of the Friar and his relationship to Romeo; acts as
confidant; awareness of the families' feuding.

PART 2

Actions he takes throughout the play: performs wedding ceremony;
comforts both Romeo and Juliet when things go wrong; arranges for
Romeo to go to Mantua; supplies drug for Juliet; attempts vainly to
save her when everything goes wrong.

PART 3

Examination of his motives – to help his friend, to reunite the families,
to preserve the marriage, to portray his actions in a favourable light.

PART 4

Explanations for his actions – he has a sense of superiority, he looks
for the regard and respect of others, he is afraid of his shortcomings
being exposed in the event of failure. But it could be argued that he is
acting out of the purest of motives – he genuinely wishes to bring an
end to the families' discord, his plans are naive since he is quite an
unworldly man, he is the unwitting instrument for the will of God.

EXAMINER'S SECRET
Don't waste time looking to see how your friends are doing!

PART 5

Others are every bit as much implicated in the deaths; he has no part in the fatal fight between Tybalt and Mercutio; the Nurse knows as much about the real events as anyone else but shies away from involvement at a key moment; the family feud eventually must lead to such a tragedy; all the characters are caught up in a sequence of events that is destined to end in the death of the lovers.

PART 6

Conclusion: the Friar is responsible for setting in motion a series of actions which lead to the couple's marriage, the arrangements for their later reunion, supplying the drug to Juliet and failing to save her from herself. His motives are genuine if misguided. Others contribute to the tragedy to a greater or lesser degree. The events are, however, fated to happen and in that sense the Friar is an innocent agent of Fate.

This is by no means an exhaustive or definitive answer to the question though it does indicate the way your mind should be working in order to achieve a reasonably thorough essay.

EXAMINER'S SECRET
Tackling sample questions such as these is good practice for the examination.

FURTHER QUESTIONS

Make a plan as shown above and attempt these questions.

1. What makes *Romeo and Juliet* such a great love story?

2. Examine the ways in which *West Side Story* converts the play into a musical.

3. Explain how the conflict is caused and how it is presented in *Romeo and Juliet*.

4. Do you think that the play has more to say to parents than to children?

5. Can Romeo and Juliet be truly in love or do you feel that it is infatuation? Justify your conclusions by close reference to the play.

6 Describe Romeo and Juliet's first meeting at the masked ball and show how Shakespeare brings out the beauty and romance of the occasion.

7 What do you think of Lord Capulet's treatment of Juliet throughout the play?

8 Do you feel that Paris is intended as a sympathetic character or not?

9 Write a letter from the Nurse to her (supposed) sister describing the events in the play.

10 Compare and contrast the behaviour of Tybalt and Benvolio in the play.

DID YOU KNOW?

Hector Berlioz gave his first performance of the *Romeo and Juliet* Symphony in 1839 – a work for solo voice, choir and orchestra.

Now take a break!

alliteration a sequence of repeated consonant sounds

antithesis opposing or contrasting ideas

Aristotle (384–322BC) the Greek philosopher who analysed tragedy and defined the characteristics of tragic drama

aubade a song at dawn, usually by a lover lamenting parting

blank verse unrhymed iambic pentameter; the commonest Shakespearean poetic form

caesura a deliberate break in rhythm in a line of verse

catastrophe the final moments of a tragedy when the plot is resolved

catharsis Aristotle's explanation that the audience's emotions are purged by the events of a tragedy enabling them to contemplate the drama in a thoughtful, calm manner

characternym a name that represents its bearer in some appropriate way

comedy a broad description for a drama which is intended primarily to entertain the audience and which ends happily for the characters

confidant(e) the trusted (fe)male friend of a main character who will listen to secrets

courtly love a type of love in which the man idealises the woman, based on the view that human love is an ennobling, even spiritual experience

denouement the clearing up of all the complications of the plot, usually as here in Romeo and Juliet in the final scene

eponym a character whose name appears in the title, e.g. Juliet

figurative language language that is not literally true, e.g. Romeo flew to Mantua

genre the term for a kind or type of literature, e.g. romantic novel, short story, play

hubris the self-confidence that enables a tragic hero to ignore the warnings of the gods and that leads to his downfall

hyperbole a figure of speech in which emphasis is achieved by exaggeration

imagery word pictures which assist understanding and interpretation. The use of images of light in the play help to underpin the theme

irony when the characters in a play are blind to fateful circumstances of which the audience is fully aware (e.g. Juliet's joyful anticipation of Romeo on their wedding night in Act III, Scene 2). It is also applied to actions that produce the desired outcome though not in the way foreseen by the character (e.g. the Friar's intention of ending the feud by marrying Romeo and Juliet)

malapropism mistaken or muddled use of long words

onomatopoeia a figure of speech in which words are used to sound like the noise they describe

oxymoron a figure of speech in which contradictory words are placed together

paradox an apparently self-contradictory statement behind which lies a truth

personification a figure of speech in which things or ideas are treated as if human

Petrarch Italian poet (1304–74) whose poetry was directed to the idealised memory of Laura, filled with highly coloured expressions of his emotions, showing the effect of love on his changing moods

prose all writings not in verse

pun a play on words

quatrain a verse consisting of four lines

rhyming couplet a pair of lines that rhyme

simile a direct comparison

soliloquy a speech given to the audience revealing thoughts, motives or decisions

sonnet a fourteen-line poetic form first popularised by Petrarch (see above), which was a major influence on European literature. Shakespeare wrote a cycle of 154 sonnets published in 1609

tragedy a drama which traces the career and downfall of an individual (see pages 8–9 for fuller description)

Checkpoint 1 Look at their differing attitudes to the fighting: Benvolio is a peacemaker, Tybalt is looking for a fight.

Checkpoint 2 Capulet is a concerned father: he is worried Juliet is too young and he wants her to agree to the marriage.

Checkpoint 3 Mercutio's speech about Queen Mab makes quite clear that unlike Romeo he sees love as mainly to do with sex.

Checkpoint 4 He agrees to go but he promises that Romeo's intrusion on the ball will lead to 'bitterest gall' (poison).

Checkpoint 5 Mercutio still believes that women and men are only interested in sexual satisfaction (lines 6–40).

Checkpoint 6 Wherefore means why.

Checkpoint 7 Romeo is prepared to joke with his friends for the first time (lines 47–91) but quickly becomes serious when he talks to the Nurse (lines 140–205).

Checkpoint 8 Look at the excitement of her soliloquy and her impatience with the Nurse.

Checkpoint 9 Mercutio listens to Romeo doing nothing about Tybalt's insults until he can take no more (lines 59–71).

Checkpoint 10 She is impatient to be with her new husband and spend the night together.

Checkpoint 11 Consider the consequences for him if their marriage became public knowledge.

Checkpoint 12 Lady Capulet naturally assumes Juliet is weeping over the death of her cousin, Tybalt.

Checkpoint 13 Look at the first scene where we met him (II, 3) when he was considering the various properties of plants.

Checkpoint 14 Friar Lawrence

Checkpoint 15 She briefly wonders if he has given her a poison to save himself from disgrace in having married her to Romeo (lines 24–29).

Checkpoint 16 Juliet is not actually dead so Shakespeare may be saving the real expression of grief for the end of the play (V, 3, lines 202–304).

Checkpoint 17 He might check with the Friar or the Nurse to see if Juliet is really dead; he could attempt to contact his family for the same purpose.

Checkpoint 18 He is worried that Juliet will be angry with him that he has not told Romeo about what has happened.

Checkpoint 19 A number of people might feel guilty about what has happened: Friar Lawrence, both the Capulets and even Balthasar.

Checkpoint 20 Prince Escalus

TEST YOURSELF (ACT I)

1 Benvolio (*1.65*)

2 Romeo (*1.173*)

3 Capulet (*2.9*)

4 Juliet (*3.95*)

5 Romeo (*5.62*)

6 Paris (*3.78*)

7 Romeo (*5.66*)

8 Mercutio (*4.97*)

TEST YOURSELF (ACT II)

1 Mercutio (*1.33*)

2 Juliet (*2.38*)

3 The Nurse (*5.75*)

4 Benvolio (*1.22*)

5 Juliet's relatives, Romeo (*2.70*)

6 Romeo (*4.87*)

7 The Nurse (*5.27*)

8 Juliet (*6.16*)

TEST YOURSELF (ACT III)

1 Benvolio (*1.4*)

2 Romeo (*1.67*)

3 Mercutio (*1.107*)

4 Juliet (*5.116*)

5 Benvolio (*1.177*)

6 Romeo (*2.22*)

7 The Nurse (*5.172*)

8 The Nurse (*5.230*)

TEST YOURSELF (ACT IV)

1 Juliet (*1.61*)

2 Friar Lawrence (*1.76*)

3 Juliet (*3.9*)

4 Juliet (*2.22*)

5 Friar Lawrence (*2.32*)

6 Juliet (*2.15*)

7 Tybalt (*3.42*)

8 Juliet (*5.26*)

TEST YOURSELF (ACT V)

1 Romeo (*1.6*)

2 Balthasar (*1.18*)

3 Romeo (*1.83*)

4 Friar John (*2.14*)

5 Romeo (*1.28*)

6 Romeo (*3.167*)

7 Juliet (*3.102*)

8 Romeo and Juliet (*3.303*)

Maya Angelou
I Know Why the Caged Bird Sings

Jane Austen
Pride and Prejudice

Alan Ayckbourn
Absent Friends

Elizabeth Barrett Browning
Selected Poems

Robert Bolt
A Man for All Seasons

Harold Brighouse
Hobson's Choice

Charlotte Brontë
Jane Eyre

Emily Brontë
Wuthering Heights

Shelagh Delaney
A Taste of Honey

Charles Dickens
David Copperfield
Great Expectations
Hard Times
Oliver Twist

Roddy Doyle
Paddy Clarke Ha Ha Ha

George Eliot
Silas Marner
The Mill on the Floss

Anne Frank
The Diary of a Young Girl

William Golding
Lord of the Flies

Oliver Goldsmith
She Stoops to Conquer

Willis Hall
The Long and the Short and the Tall

Thomas Hardy
Far from the Madding Crowd

The Mayor of Casterbridge
Tess of the d'Urbervilles
The Withered Arm and other Wessex Tales

L.P. Hartley
The Go-Between

Seamus Heaney
Selected Poems

Susan Hill
I'm the King of the Castle

Barry Hines
A Kestrel for a Knave

Louise Lawrence
Children of the Dust

Harper Lee
To Kill a Mockingbird

Laurie Lee
Cider with Rosie

Arthur Miller
The Crucible
A View from the Bridge

Robert O'Brien
Z for Zachariah

Frank O'Connor
My Oedipus Complex and Other Stories

George Orwell
Animal Farm

J.B. Priestley
An Inspector Calls
When We Are Married

Willy Russell
Educating Rita
Our Day Out

J.D. Salinger
The Catcher in the Rye

William Shakespeare
Henry IV Part I
Henry V
Julius Caesar

Macbeth
The Merchant of Venice
A Midsummer Night's Dream
Much Ado About Nothing
Romeo and Juliet
The Tempest
Twelfth Night

George Bernard Shaw
Pygmalion

Mary Shelley
Frankenstein

R.C. Sherriff
Journey's End

Rukshana Smith
Salt on the snow

John Steinbeck
Of Mice and Men

Robert Louis Stevenson
Dr Jekyll and Mr Hyde

Jonathan Swift
Gulliver's Travels

Robert Swindells
Daz 4 Zoe

Mildred D. Taylor
Roll of Thunder, Hear My Cry

Mark Twain
Huckleberry Finn

James Watson
Talking in Whispers

Edith Wharton
Ethan Frome

William Wordsworth
Selected Poems

A Choice of Poets

Mystery Stories of the Nineteenth Century including The Signalman

Nineteenth Century Short Stories

Poetry of the First World War

Six Women Poets

Margaret Atwood
Cat's Eye
The Handmaid's Tale

Jane Austen
Emma
Mansfield Park
Persuasion
Pride and Prejudice
Sense and Sensibility

Alan Bennett
Talking Heads

William Blake
Songs of Innocence and of Experience

Charlotte Brontë
Jane Eyre
Villette

Emily Brontë
Wuthering Heights

Angela Carter
Nights at the Circus

Geoffrey Chaucer
The Franklin's Prologue and Tale
The Miller's Prologue and Tale
The Prologue to the Canterbury Tales
The Wife of Bath's Prologue and Tale

Samuel Coleridge
Selected Poems

Joseph Conrad
Heart of Darkness

Daniel Defoe
Moll Flanders

Charles Dickens
Bleak House
Great Expectations
Hard Times

Emily Dickinson
Selected Poems

John Donne
Selected Poems

Carol Ann Duffy
Selected Poems

George Eliot
Middlemarch
The Mill on the Floss

T.S. Eliot
Selected Poems
The Waste Land

F. Scott Fitzgerald
The Great Gatsby

E.M. Forster
A Passage to India

Brian Friel
Translations

Thomas Hardy
Jude the Obscure
The Mayor of Casterbridge
The Return of the Native
Selected Poems
Tess of the d'Urbervilles

Seamus Heaney
Selected Poems from 'Opened Ground'

Nathaniel Hawthorne
The Scarlet Letter

Homer
The Iliad
The Odyssey

Aldous Huxley
Brave New World

Kazuo Ishiguro
The Remains of the Day

Ben Jonson
The Alchemist

James Joyce
Dubliners

John Keats
Selected Poems

Christopher Marlowe
Doctor Faustus
Edward II

Arthur Miller
Death of a Salesman

John Milton
Paradise Lost Books I & II

Toni Morrison
Beloved

George Orwell
Nineteen Eighty-Four

Sylvia Plath
Selected Poems

Alexander Pope
Rape of the Lock & Selected Poems

William Shakespeare
Antony and Cleopatra
As You Like It
Hamlet
Henry IV Part I
King Lear
Macbeth
Measure for Measure
The Merchant of Venice
A Midsummer Night's Dream
Much Ado About Nothing
Othello
Richard II
Richard III
Romeo and Juliet
The Taming of the Shrew
The Tempest
Twelfth Night
The Winter's Tale

George Bernard Shaw
Saint Joan

Mary Shelley
Frankenstein

Jonathan Swift
Gulliver's Travels and A Modest Proposal

Alfred Tennyson
Selected Poems

Virgil
The Aeneid

Alice Walker
The Color Purple

Oscar Wilde
The Importance of Being Earnest

Tennessee Williams
A Streetcar Named Desire

Jeanette Winterson
Oranges Are Not the Only Fruit

John Webster
The Duchess of Malfi

Virginia Woolf
To the Lighthouse

W.B. Yeats
Selected Poems

Metaphysical Poets